DEATH VALLEY
PROSPECTORS

DEATH VALLEY PROSPECTORS

 *by* Dane Coolidge

Sagebrush Press ❧
P. O. Box 87 • Morongo Valley, Calif. 92256
1985

Library of Congress Catalog Card No. 85-62283
isbn 0-930704-17-7 (Trade Edition)
isbn 0-930704-18-5 (Deluxe Edition)

Printed in the United States of America

Publisher's Introduction

This new edition of *Death Valley Prospectors* is being issued almost 50 years since it originally appeared in 1937. Even though the world has witnessed radical change in the ensuing decades, these writings of another era still carry interesting narrative and dialogue that bring commemorative as well as instructive enjoyment to the reader. And while Death Valley in some respects has also undergone great change, the environment and back-country remains as it has for hundreds of years. And if one's imagination is attuned to the voice of the wilderness, stories such as these told by Dane Coolidge will bring some of those earlier times into focus once again.

Dane Coolidge the author (1875-1940) ranked foremost as a novelist, in the same league as Zane Grey, but not with the public acclaim accorded the latter. It was Coolidge's novels of Western America that carried great appeal to a large clientele, but it was his non-fiction works such as *Fighting Men of the West* (1932) and *Death Valley Prospectors* that triggered the attention of a whole new panorama of readers. In these works personalities of the Old West were captured in the pages of books to be read, back then as well as in current times. Here are grass-root stories from a land that offered scant foliage, sun-baked information of man and beast who trekked the salt plains of the desert, lusty tales both factual and stretched, stories that today tell us about those earlier years in Death Valley.

Any library that features Death Valley books and stories will require several feet of shelf space, and to such a collection this new edition will be justifiably added. In addition to a complete new design and typographical format, a workable index not found in the original edition has been incorporated at the book's conclusion. This helpful tool will enable the reader to find quickly an elusive name or place in the text, a time-saving feature for all, except those with photographic memories.

The pages ahead tell about the original emigrants who sought a short cut to the gold fields of California; the Shoshone Indians of the region; borax and how it drew the attention of the world to this forbidden place; Breyfogle and his "lost mine"; the violent and short career of Panamint City; and of four enduring characters who called the Valley their home.

The reader is invited to note still an extra feature in this edition, an insight into the life and times of Dane Coolidge, found on page 119. By marriage, Nancy Coolidge Coulter was a niece to the author, and in her "I Remember Dane Coolidge" she provides a pleasant look back to the days when she recalls the man and his equally talented wife, Mary. This delightful vignette was written in July of 1985 when this new edition was in preparation, and it thereby offers a fresh and brisk look at the man and his time as seen a half century ago.

— Daniel L. Cronkhite
Sagebrush Press

Contents

Illustrations

➤ This new edition of *Death Valley Prospectors* has been composed in Linotype Baskerville, for the text, with handset Egyptian and Times-Roman used in the composition of the title page and chapter headings. Reproduction proofs have been pulled from the "hot metal" type forms and lithographic presswork employed to produce 2,000 copies of the trade edition (in wrappers) and 250 clothbound copies of the deluxe edition. ✔

DEATH VALLEY
PROSPECTORS

Chapter One

"White Ones Coming!"

It was on Christmas Day, 1849, that the first white men gazed on Death Valley. They came down Furnace Creek with their wagons; and the Indians, camped below, were scared. Never in their lives had they seen a white man. They had never seen cattle—horses—wagons. Nobody knew what these strange things were that were lumbering down the canyon and Hungry Bill, the son of their war chief, cried out:

"White ones coming!"

Then they all turned and ran.

There were two bands of Shoshones at the mouth of Furnace Creek where the water, flowing out into the Valley, formed two great thickets of mesquite trees, with patches of reeds along the marsh. It was their winter home, where they built round houses of tules and gathered mesquite beans and seeds. They caught kangaroo rats in deadfalls and ate them, and trapped coyotes for their furs. But now they fled, leaving everything—and one old man, who was blind.

He was Hungry Bill's grandfather, a man so old that he crawled on his hands and knees like an animal. William Manly, who entered the Valley the next day, found his strange-looking tracks by a cave and followed them to a well-like hole which had been excavated in the sand-hills. Looking down he could see a kind of Indian mummy, curled up like a dog in the bottom.

"He was not dead for I could see him move as he breathed,

[*13*]

but his skin looked very much like the surface of a well-dried vension ham. I should think by his looks he must be 200 or 300 years old."

As the strangers took possession of their camps, the Shoshones fled clear to the Panamint Mountains, miles away across Death Valley; but that night the old man's daughter crept in and asked him how they had treated him.

"They feed me good," he said. "I feel fine."

After the white people left, his daughter came and looked for him again, but he had got lost in crawling around and when she found him he was dead from the cold.

These white wagons were the first of the Sand-Walking Company, on their way to the gold fields of California. While heading south, from Salt Lake City to San Bernardino, they had heard of a short-cut to the west; and now, like the old Indian, they were hopelessly lost but still struggling blindly on.

In the lead of these twenty-seven wagons was a band of adventurers called the Jayhawkers. They were all active young men, having no women or children in their party; but behind them followed seven wagons containing families, who proceeded at a slower pace. It was to this party that the scout, William Manly, belonged; and from his book *Death Valley in '49* we get most of the details regarding the fate of the white men.

The Indian side of the story was told to me by Tom Wilson, a Shoshone who married the daughter of Hungry Bill and got it from her father. At the time the emigrants came, Hungry Bill was a boy of twelve, but he lived to be nearly a hundred, having died only a few years ago.

The Shoshones are a small but warlike tribe, claiming all the Death Valley country from the summit of the Funeral Range to the land of the Paiutes, in Owens Valley. To the east is another tribe of Paiutes—another people, speaking a different language—the mortal enemies of the Shoshones, with whom they were constantly at war. The summit of the Funeral Range is the deadline between these two tribes and any warrior who ventured over it was, until very recently, killed.

On account of their peculiar isolation in this wild and desert land the Shoshones had never seen the Mexicans, who lived along the coast. They had never seen a gun nor matched their wits against the white man's, but as the Jayhawkers moved north toward Salt Creek in their efforts to cross Death Valley, the Indians took courage and followed them.

For many years the story has been told of the death of this heroic band—how they drank the poison waters of Salt Creek and perished almost to a man. But now the younger Indians agree with Manly that they did not die there at all. The water of Salt Creek is indeed poisonous, containing Glauber and Epsom salts; but the Shoshones—who were believed to have watched them die if they did not actually kill them—claim they abandoned their wagons and went on.

The early story of the death of these emigrants came straight enough from Panamint Tom himself, chief of the Shoshone or Panamint Indians. But Tom, during his lifetime, had had trouble with the white men over his weakness for killing prospectors; and when he told it to his friend Dad Fairbanks of Shoshone, he diverged somewhat from the truth. However, as it has become the standard account, it is given as told by Fairbanks.

"Tom said the emigrants were badly scared. They separated at Furnace Creek and the greater number moved north to Salt Creek. It was in the heat of summer and at Salt Creek they let the oxen drink the bad water, not knowing that it was poison.

"The Shoshones followed them at a distance and gathered on the black buttes across the Valley, near Tucki Mountain, where they watched the people below. Tom said it was not the bad water that killed them, but fear. The Shoshones did not attack them; but they were in sight, looking down from the mountain, and the people went crazy. Many oxen died and the heat was terrible. On the second day the people ran around in circles. On the third day all who remained with the wagons were dead. 'Then everything was ours.'

"The Indians looted the wagons and liked the meat and sugar, but could find no use for the flour. They tried it for painting their faces but it caked and came off, so the women threw it all out to get the sacks. Several of this Jayhawker party escaped, going up the wash to Emigrant Spring, and the Indians did not attack them. They already had lots of horses and cattle and the loot from the wagons, including a great deal of clothing and calico. Nor did the Indians molest the Bennett Party, which had gone south down the Valley, although they could have killed them if they had wanted to. They were poor and had nothing, anyhow."

Panamint Tom was Dad Fairbanks' first guide into Death Valley, along about 1903. He had a name as a killer and Fairbanks said to him:

"This is your country, Tom. You know all the trails, so you go ahead."

This kept the old chief up in front, where Dad could watch him. At night he always let Tom make his bed down first, then made his own bed where he could watch him. After they became friendly, Tom showed him the cave in Johnson's Canyon where he was born. It is one of two, halfway up the Panamint Mountains from Hungry Bill's ranch. Tom's grandfather and grandmother are buried near there, so they have occupied the country for a century, at least.

Tom said that the Shoshones were from the north. There was dissension in the tribe and his people came south. At one time there were several hundred of them; but at Shoshone a disease, probably small-pox, killed off a great number and they moved further west, into the Panamint Range. They lived by hunting mountain sheep and raising corn and vegetables where there was water.

Told under such circumstances, Panamint Tom's story was

accepted as the truth; but both Manly's book and the account of Tom Wilson, Hungry Bill's son-in-law, show that the emigrants perished in the winter-time, when it was cold enough to freeze the old grandfather. They also agree in the fact that the Jayhawkers did not perish at Salt Creek but left their wagons there, packed their oxen with dried meat and went on towards the west. Manly himself met their leader, Doty, on his forced march to reach the settlements; and in later years he found many more of them who had survived their arduous trip.

Now that Panamint Tom and Hungry Bill are dead and beyond the reach of any punishment, Tom Wilson has consented to tell the real story, just as it was told to him by his grandparents.

"My grandmother and her people were camped at Surveyors' Well, a few miles north of Salt Creek, and she says the white people camped there for several days before they started west. They killed three or four oxen and burned a wagon to smoke the meat. Then they took all the stock and struck out on foot. On the east side of the summit, the white people threw away their coats and blankets, took all their food and went ahead.

"When the Indians visited the abandoned camp they found only one dead man. There were not a lot of dead people—just one man who had broken his leg and had been shot through the forehead and body. The Jayhawkers had gone away without burying him. My grandmother used to tell how runners came down to Pine Nut and summoned the other Indians to Salt Creek. The wagons were full of fine things—blankets and clothes and pieces of iron, the first metal they had ever seen. They burned all the woodwork to get possession of it, using the long irons to dig holes in the ground whenever they built a new brush house."

Chapter Two

The Bennett Party

The Bennett Party, of which William Lewis Manly was guide, scout and historian, was composed of seven wagons which had been left behind by the Jayhawkers. They were all family men, unattached to any party, and followed along without any fixed purpose. They did not even travel together, but dragged along, every man for himself, often shunning the others entirely.

The one group which stuck together—and escaped—were the families of Asabel Bennett and J. B. Arcane; and to this was attached John Rogers and Manly, whose book *Death Valley in '49* was the first published description of the trip. Without these two young men the entire party would have perished miserably; but by a forced march they went ahead to the settlements, returning with horses and food in time to save them all. The rest of the party, who had become tired of waiting, were never heard from again.

Forty years later, while a prosperous agriculturist at San Jose, William Manly wrote down his terrible experiences, showing himself to be a capable historian as well as a true friend and a brave scout. Thirteen of the original party lie unburied along the trail and, but for one of the wettest winters ever known—which forced the rain-clouds over the high mountains and filled the few water-holes that saved them—the entire expedition would have been lost.

After the twenty wagons of the Jayhawkers had gone by

Furnace Creek and turned north, the Bennett party came down the wash and struck out to the south. Finding their way blocked by the marshes of Bad Water, they crossed Death Valley on the solid salt and kept on down the western side. Then they swung around and came back, seeking a way out through the canyons to the west, until they settled down at Bennett's Well.

This water-hole had long been used by the Indians, who scraped out the sand, filled their pitch-covered water-baskets and covered the hole again to keep the water clean. Though the emigrants did not know it, they were under constant observation from the time they arrived at the well, the family of Hungry Bill being camped less than a mile away in the shelter of the sand-hills, where it was warmer.

The Bennett Party was hopelessly lost—and had been since they quit their Mormon guide and tried to make a short-cut west. For two hundred miles they had seen the snowy summit of the Panamints ahead of them and thought they were the Sierra Nevada Mountains. Having read Fremont's travels they felt sure that, on the other side of this peak, there lay a beautiful country, rich in cattle and horses—in fact, California.

On the eastern side of this mountain range, Fremont had said, the country was barren, dry and rocky, a sandy desert as far as the eye could see; and that they knew to be true. What they did not realize was the width of this barren zone, which cut them off from the promised land where the soil was full of gold. They did not doubt yet that, once over this snowy summit, they would come out in "California."

For a month they had been plodding west across the worst desert in America and when they halted at Bennett's Well their oxen were so weak they lay down under the yoke. That night they talked the matter over and the next morning the four teamsters who had been driving the oxen decided to follow the trail of the Jayhawkers, as promising them a better chance for their lives. They were given what provisions they could carry and struck out north on foot, leaving the others to their fate.

Down-hearted and weak the Bennett Party yoked up their famished oxen and toiled up a rocky canyon to the west until at last they were stopped by a solid wall of stone, which could be ascended only on foot. Manly went ahead and, from a high peak, looked out the country beyond; and as far as the eye could see there was no sign of water, nothing but an endless desert. When he hurried back to the people he found them without a drop of water and with nothing for the oxen to eat. Even with a down-hill pull they could barely drag the wagons back to Bennett's Well, where they sank down in the sand, exhausted.

That night they had another meeting to determine what should be done, and it was evident they must abandon everything and think only of saving their lives. It was finally decided to send Manly and Rogers ahead to seek a settlement and food, while the two families remained at Bennett's Well and waited for their return. An ox was killed for the meat, moccasins were made out of the rawhide and the women made each scout a knapsack. Then, while Mrs. Bennett asked God to bless them and send back food for her starving children, they turned back up the canyon.

From the summit of the Panamint Range they looked on a level plain to the south; but, far to the west, they could dimly see another range of mountains whose peaks were covered with snow. It was the Sierra Nevadas, over a hundred miles away, and they sat down to decide what to do. They knew that to go over the summit of these mountains and return in fifteen days was impossible, but the lives of the women and children had been placed in their hands and it was up to them to try.

Down the steep slope they hurried towards the two rocky ranges ahead and in the valley below they came to a clear stream of water, flowing slowly towards a lake. But when they rushed to slake their thirst they found it as salt as brine. They now began the ascent of the Slate Range and, near its summit, they found the trail of the Jayhawkers, who had evidently been forced to the south. They had camped here and had dug holes in the sand for water, but had found none. A short distance down the trail they found the body of Mr. Fish, from whom they had parted not two weeks before.

Suffering greatly from thirst, they followed the Jayhawker trail to the next valley, which opened out to the south, revealing the wide expanse of what is now Searles Lake, whose wine-colored water was undrinkable. Turning west again they ascended the Argus Range, finding an Indian hut but no water; and so they went on again. Early the next morning they found a skim of ice which had frozen during the night, and gathered enough to fill their canteens with water before the sun rose and melted it.

Seeing the rocky bluff of the Southern Sierras ahead they walked all day without reaching their base, but as the sun went down they saw a small smoke there and came upon a camp of the Jayhawkers under Captain Doty. They had stopped to dry the meat of an ox that had given out, and near at hand there was a spring. There were others of their party ahead, following a trail which led over the mountains to the west. It was every man for himself, but they gave Manly and Rogers some meat and showed them a worn trail which they had sworn to follow if it went clear to Mexico.

These men were greatly discouraged, having been without water for four or five days at a time, but when told of the women and children who waited for the scouts to return they gave them a supply of dried beef and sent them on their way. Further down the trail they overtook the advance party of the Jayhawkers, who had turned off on a trail leading south. There they found the four teamsters who had abandoned Bennett and Arcane, and already they were out of grub, with no way of getting any more. When the Jayhawkers killed an ox they humbly begged for the poorest parts and thus far had kept alive.

Manly and Rogers divided up their meat and gave them some; for, although an ox had been killed that day, they had not been able to get a mouthful. The whole camp was silent, for before them was a level plain, which had the appearance of being so broad as to take five or six days to cross. Passing on, ahead of the advance guard of Jayhawkers, the scouts went through what was probably Red Rock Canyon and came out in the Mojave Desert, which stretched before them, endlessly.

But, only three or four miles from the hills, they came to a tall bunch of willows which surrounded a spring of good water—probably Cane Springs—and stopped for a last drink and to fill their canteens before they followed the old trail south and west. Here for the first time they found the skulls of many horses, which had perished while crossing the desert and before they reached the spring. It was evidently the end of the old Paiute war-trail; where the Indians, after raiding the settlements, came in driving their stolen stock home.

For a man on foot, this trail in an ordinary season would have meant death—over a hundred miles across the desert, without a single spring. But the winter of '49 and '50 was an exceptionally wet one and, after losing their trail in the drifting sand, they found a little pond of rain-water and so reached the other side. First they shot a crow, then a hawk, then a quail; and after eating these their strength was sufficient to take them over the mountains.

There a beautiful scene spread out before them. There were running brooks, broad fields covered with cattle and horses, tall cottonwoods and oaks; but no sign of human habitations. In desperation they killed a fat yearling, dried the meat and started on; until at last they were made welcome by the native Californians, whom they had imagined to be desperate characters. They were taken in and fed and provided with horses and provisions, and when a Mexican woman learned that there were four children in Death Valley she sent them out four oranges.

[*23*]

With two horses and a mule, a sack of beans and a quantity of flour and dried meat, Manly and Rogers set out on their return trip without waiting to regain their strength. They had agreed to return within fifteen days, but it seemed very likely it would take twenty-five or thirty—and the Bennetts, in their desperation, might try to follow after them, might take some other trail and get lost. In their weakened condition they would never survive the journey. It was necessary to reach them at once.

Travelling fast across the wide expanse of desert, they retraced their steps to the Panamint Mountains. Across their summit lay Death Valley and their friends, but could a horse mount the dizzy heights? They turned up a narrow canyon, it grew rougher and more shut in, until at last they were faced by a high wall of slippery rock which only the mule could mount. Leaving their horses to die they clambered up after the little mule and continued their mad dash for the wagons. But when at last they sighted them, nothing moved. Not a soul was in sight.

It had been twenty-five days since Manly and Rogers had departed, and everything was changed. Instead of seven wagons they could see only four, and these had been stripped of their canvas. Ever since the emigrants had robbed a Paiute camp, far to the east, Manly had feared an Indian attack. Now it seemed as if, in his absence, the Bennetts had been killed. Even then the blood-thirsty savages might be waiting to kill them, too.

Within a hundred yards of the wagons he fired off his gun. There was silence, a long wait. Then a man appeared, more heads popped up—they saw the children. Mr. Bennett threw his arms up and shouted:

"The boys have come!"

They were saved and made their way out to the settlements. The others who had left them all perished.

[*24*]

Chapter Three

Burnt Wagons

Of the twenty-seven wagons that left the big train to seek a short-cut to the west, not one ever reached the settlements. They were abandoned and burned, either to spite the Indians or to cover up the graves of the dead. To cover up hidden treasure, even—and, since the first white men came into the country, the search for it has never ceased. Mysterious strangers have turned up, with maps given them by survivors, and traced the dimmed trails to where piles of old iron marked the burning-place of some wagon.

In the early days the abandoned ox-chains were carted away and used for logging. Now a good length of ox-chain would be worth hundreds of dollars—a good ox-yoke is worth a hundred and fifty. But the piles of old iron were not what the strangers sought. There was a jeweler on one of those wagons, and when he died they buried his treasure with him, and burned a wagon to hide the grave.

Herman Jones, of Shoshone, is an authority on the burnt wagons. He has traced out three roads over the washed boulders of the pass where the hurrying white men, after a fight with the Indians, pushed on over the divide west of Death Valley Junction and down into the Valley itself. These roads, made in 1849, are as clear to his experienced eye as if they had been broken yesterday. Where they passed over the wash-boulders, the tires left red marks on the rocks; and where they crossed the smooth, level ground the wheel-tracks are sunk deep in the soil.

It is a country where nothing changes—unless another cloud-burst comes along; and a hundred years from now the wagon-tracks of the Jayhawkers will still lead on up the pass. But in the last few years all the ox-yokes and old iron have been collected by acquisitive tourists. For years, at the place marked Lost Wagons on the map, an old trail-wagon with one broken wheel stood just where the teamster of a borax-wagon had dropped it, in the upper reaches of Lost Valley. Now it is a treasured relic at Stove-pipe Wells Hotel and Lost Wagons has been wiped off the map.

One of the earliest settlers in the Death Valley country, and one of the first to collect old iron, was Dad Fairbanks of Baker, California. He has quite a collection of old lynch-pins and wagon-hounds, hub-bands and hand-hammered body-bolts; and long ago he sent an ox-chain home for his people to use snaking logs. He found the burnt wagons with the aid of his old friend, Ash Meadows Charley, the war chief of the Paiutes at the time when the emigrants crossed. His account of the fighting, and the causes which led up to it, is given in the words of Fairbanks:

"Death Valley got its name from a big party of emigrants who perished there in 1849. They had come from Salt Lake City over the Mormon Trail, but originally they were from Illinois. At Salt Lake they engaged a regular Mormon guide, but near Las Vegas they split up and the guide quit. Part of the wagon-train wanted to continue south by way of the Mormon Trail to San Bernardino, but the rest had heard of a short-cut across the desert to the Sierras, and started out by themselves. Those who kept on arrived safely at San Bernardino.

"At Indian Spring, about forty miles northwest of Las Vegas, the short-cut emigrants found fields of corn, pumpkins and beans which the Paiutes had planted, and took all they want-ed, paying nothing. When the Indians protested they drove them off, and the Paiutes claim they abused some of their women. I got this account from the Indians themselves, especially from Ash Meadows Charley, who lived to be over a hundred years old and was chief of the Ash Meadows Paiutes.

"After the emigrants had gone on, the Indian Creek Indians held a council and decided to follow them, to get revenge. They picked up the Ash Meadows Paiutes and together they followed the wagon-train to a place now called Burnt Wagons, about seven miles north-west of Death Valley Junction, on the old road that followed the railroad. There, while the emigrants were encamped, the Indians sneaked up in the night and drove off a lot of oxen and horses.

"The white men pursued them on horseback and, as the Indians could not drive the oxen away, they killed a great number of them and escaped with quite a few horses. They were armed with bows and arrows and a few guns; but the emigrants whipped them off, although a few white men were killed. Herman Jones says that one of these was a jeweler from Missouri, who had six hundred dollars in silver, besides a great many jewels and watches.

"On account of so many oxen having been killed, the emigrants threw away a great weight of ox-chains and old iron in order to lighten their loads, and besides had to abandon several wagons. Two holes were dug and in one the jeweler was buried. In the other his money and jewelry was hidden and, over the two graves, the wagons were burned, so the Indians would not find them.

"Jones worked on Ash Meadows Charley a long time, claiming the man who had died was his uncle. He wanted to find his body so he could dig it up and bury it back east in the family graveyard, but Charley knew what he was looking for.

"Yes! Maybeso money!" he said; and from that Herman knew that the Indians had found the grave.

"Jones got the story of the jeweler from an old man from San Bernardino, who many years later spent six months looking around in the neighborhood of Burnt Wagons. According to this old man's tale the jeweler was moving west, taking with him his entire stock of watches and jewels as well as six hundred dollars in silver. The stranger had been given a map of the place by some man who was dying down in Mexico. He had hunted a long time without explaining his purpose, but before he went home he told Herman what he had been looking for."

This story of hidden treasure set Jones to looking. He was conducting a road-house at Nelson's Well, three miles northwest of Death Valley Junction, and in his spare time he took up the search. Jones knew that the wagons had gone out through the pass into Death Valley, and that they would follow the line of least resistance—that is, keep down in the wash and out of the rocks and gulches. So he laid the country off in swaths, by tying white rags on the bushes, each line parallel to the main wash. He would walk the length of the main swath with his eye on a peak ahead, then step over a short distance and return.

In this way he found Burnt Wagons—in what was then a low place to the right of the main wash, going up it. At that time there were a lot of tires and hounds lying about; and, about half a mile north, he found an ox-yoke, which is now in a Salt Lake Museum. Most of this old iron and the ox-chains were carried off later by the settlers; and, during the rush to Skidoo, the new road went right by it, so that the miners got the rest.

Nothing was done to mark the spot, which lies in a big swale miles in width; and when, in 1928, Dad Fairbanks was taken to look for it he was unable to locate the place. The next day, in company with Herman Jones, we returned to continue the search; and he, by not trying to find it at all but letting his subconscious mind work, walked directly to the spot. It lies about two hundred feet to the right of the main wash going up, and a little over three miles from Nelson's Well.

We found the king-bolts and king-bolt plates of three wagons, besides some hand-made bolts and staples; and, where the old iron had formerly lain, a deep hole in the ground where Jones had been digging for the treasure. A search near the place revealed the remnants of an old metal trunk, with a key-hole shaped something like a saw-edge. Evidently the Indians had dug up the jeweler's trunk and looted it of its treasure.

Dad Fairbanks had been led to this same place five years before Herman Jones had found it, and by his old friend Ash Meadows Charley, who had told him the Indian's side of the story. But nothing was said then about the treasure or the trunk, which must have been dug up later.

After whipping off the Paiutes and burning several of their wagons the emigrants went west down the Death Valley Junction Wash. As the Funeral Range was the boundary line of the Shoshones, the Paiutes had turned back, well satisfied with killing so many oxen, whose skeletons were visible years afterward. It is the theory of Herman Jones that there were three successive parties of emigrants, but on this point Dad Fairbanks is positive there was only one. Some of the Jayhawkers were hurrying ahead, the Bennett Party followed later, and the Reverend Brier was a law unto himself, taking any road he chose.

After we had located Burnt Wagons and put up a monument, Herman Jones returned later and found another burnt wagon, several miles further to the north. And when *he* was satisfied H. L. Gower, the Superintendent for the Borax Company at Death Valley Junction, went out and found more iron, which indicates still another burnt wagon.

Herman Jones has a different story to tell of the fighting along the way, which he got from Ash Meadows Charley.

"At Corn Creek and Indian Spring the emigrants offended the Paiutes by taking their corn and punkins and booting them around when they asked for pay. These Indians called in others and, under Ash Meadows Charley, they attacked them in the night at Longstreet Spring, shooting their oxen with arrows. It was a day's journey from there to Burnt Wagons; and the Paiutes, who had been keeping them in sight, attacked again the following night. It must have taken the emigrants more than another day to get to Furnace Creek, and there they were in the country of the Shoshones, who just watched them till they died. Then they looted their wagons of everything."

Chapter Four

The Shoshone Indians

The early Shoshones did not have a very good name with the white people, principally because of the activities of Panamint Tom, their war-chief, and his brother, Hungry Bill. They were warriors of the old school and seem to have made a business of killing off stray prospectors to get their burros and supplies. But, long before Death Valley was invaded by gold-hunters, they satisfied their urge to raid by stealing horses from the settlers near Los Angeles.

Their exploits are related with some pride by Tom Wilson, who names no names but simply tells of two brothers who for many years kept the Shoshones in horse-meat. They did not sell the horses but simply gave them to their people to eat, a horse for every band.

"These men were raised in the Panamint Mountains. Went down past Barstow to big mountain, east of Los Angeles. Baldy Mountain—hunting deer. Paiutes lived down that way. They met them coming back—had five head of horses.

" 'Where you get them horses?' they asked.

" 'Way down there, close to ocean.'

" 'What you do—buy them?'

" 'No. Just go down, steal them horses.'

"After that, Shoshones talking about going down there, stealing horses. So they went down. Went to top of Baldy Mountain, by Los Angeles, so could look down. Couple days, they went down to Los Angeles. Hiding around in brush. How they going get them horses out of there? When night come, they went down there. They see two horses, tied up in high grass. So they take two—to look for more afterwards. Found another one — had one horse each. Rode them two — went out and brought off a bunch.

"During night crossed that valley. Just as sun come up they counted them horses. Thirteen head. Take two or three days get them to Panamint Valley, where lived Shoshones. When they got back, killed one each camp—lots of meat.

"Two years after, they went out again—same bunch. They went to same corral, get three saddle-horses out of it. Located bunch of horses in daytime. When they get these saddle-horses they ride out and drive off big bunch. Cross that big mountain —same as before. Sun come up—count them horses. Twenty-five head.

"Three days from there to where Ballarat is now. Warm Springs, below Indian Ranch. Count all Indians, give one to each band. What left then, sell 'em afterwards. Some Shoshones come from Death Valley—buy horse. They went to Los Angeles every year. One time six men went down. Good men. Light. Good runners—good riders.

"That time didn't go same place. They watch from hills. Lots of horses, tied up. Night comes. They went down there, got six horses. Rode down and drove off big bunch. At foot of hills when daylight come. Passed camp of other Indians—kind live in that country. Indians get after them, going take away them horses.

"Indians from here not afraid them Indians—they didn't have nothing but bows and arrows. Shoshones led by two brothers —good to dodge arrows. They go in front. Shoshones holding horses behind. Two brothers stay in lead, never move. On foot—to fight.

"Other chief come close, ready to fight. Two brothers stay same place. Come up real close—other Indian chief dodge their arrows. Two brothers snap bow-string, like shoot. Fool

(Photograph by Dane Coolidge)

DEATH VALLEY SCOTTY, 1918

PANAMINT TOM—War Chief of the Shoshones, who saw the emigrants die.

DAD FAIRBANKS OF SHOSHONE—A Friend of the Indians.

(*Photographs by Dane Coolidge*)

LOST WAGONS—Abandoned trail wagon in Lost Valley

(Photograph by Dane Coolidge)

MABEL BILL, DAUGHTER OF HUNGRY BILL—NOW MRS. TOM WILSON.

(Photograph by Dane Coolidge)

that chief, he dodge. They shoot him in stomach. Then they quit there, bring them horse Panamint Valley. Forty-seven head.

"Didn't go down then, two years. Them two brothers went again—just two. Hunted deer, Baldy Mountain, two months. Waiting for spring, and grass. Went west of Los Angeles. Hiding in brush, four days. Looking for horses. Saw white people round up horses at sundown. Big corral. Bull tied up at night, by gate. Maybeso drive horse-thief away.

"Two brothers kill bull, went into barn, get saddle horses. One drove horses out, other stay outside corral. Big bunch of horses, drove them all night. Daylight—top of mountain. When they cross big flat, noon. One hundred seventeen head. Come through Granite Well, new trail. Brought them horses to Panamint Valley. Other side of Valley, to Warm Springs.

"Big Indian camp, near Ballarat. Eleven bands, killed eleven horses—big feast. Eight more camps, further on. Killed eight more. Twenty-one camps. Warm Springs. Killed twenty-one. Kept rest and traded to other Indians. Last time them brothers go down. People in Los Angeles kill lots of Indians. Other kind of Indians. For steal horses."

That was the kind of Indians they were—Panamint Tom and Hungry Bill. They were big, tall men, and Tom had a rather pleasant cast of countenance; but Hungry Bill looked the killer he was. He was dangerous. One time when Herman Jones was prospecting near Hungry Bill's Ranch he found an old telescope, and lots of other plunder that an Indian would have no use for. And Hungry Bill claimed that country for himself.

Once Herman Jones took John Scott, a Paiute prospector, across Death Valley and into the Panamints, where Scott was going to show him a mine. He had been chopping wood near the World Beater Mine and claimed he had found a ledge of gold there and felled a tree to cover it up. But when they headed up Johnson's Canyon towards Hungry Bill's Ranch,

Scott got scared and wanted to turn back. He didn't say why, so Jones had no mercy on him—put him up in front and told him to go on.

They camped near Bill's ranch and when Scott saw him coming he lay down and covered his face with his arms. Hungry Bill came up and began to curse him for coming into his country. Bill had worked for the Mexicans at Coso and got the idea of sovereignty from them. Then he began to kick and beat the Indian, but Scott would not look up or resist. All at once Bill let out a yell and drew his knife. He had recognized John Scott as a man who had stolen one of their women and taken her to Nevada, where she had died. So Bill was going to kill him.

He jumped to stab him, but Jones drew his gun and stopped him.

"No," he said. "This man is taking me up to show me a mine, and how can he do that if he is dead?"

He finally bluffed the old Indian out, but told him if Scott didn't show him the mine he could go ahead and punish him. This put John Scott up on his toes, but the gold turned out to be iron pyrites. On the way back Scott explained that the woman had run away with another man when they got to Nevada, and when this man killed her Scott refused to complete his payment of ponies. So the Shoshones had sworn to kill him, but Herman Jones got him away.

Quite a number of men have gone into Death Valley and never been seen again, especially when they stopped at Bennett's Well, where the band of Hungry Bill camped. A posse finally rounded up Hungry Bill's band at Wild Rose Canyon, when he was returning from a raid; and its leader, Frank Kennedy, gave him a last warning, after which he changed his ways. Otherwise he might have shared the fate of the Paiutes, who were driven out of Owens Valley by the whites and many of them killed.

A great many white men came to Death Valley to hide. They

were either fugitives from justice or trying to escape private vengeance. When Dad Fairbanks first entered the country there were only five white men in it, and they were all on the dodge for something. Several were there on account of trouble at home and most of them settled down and married an Indian woman, who was easier to get along with. There was absolutely no law of any kind until a very few years ago, and the Shoshones are to be excused if they killed off a few white men in those harum-scarum days. Because most of those men needed killing.

In the winter the Shoshones came down out of the mountains and lived in Death Valley, where it was warm. There was one camp at Surveyors' Well, two at Furnace Creek and another near Bennett's Well. They brought down sacks of seeds and pinyon-nuts from the hills and gathered mesquite beans and tules in the Valley. They also trapped wood-rats and kangaroo-rats in deadfalls, made by propping up a flat rock on figure-four sticks. To catch coyotes and foxes they set a circle of rocks on edge. Then two men lifted a heavy flat rock and set it on top of the circle, supported by figure-four sticks which were baited with the body of a rat.

On the high peaks, such as Tucki, they hunted mountain sheep with bows and poisoned arrows. The poison was made from the sheep's own blood, left to rot inside the outer covering of a heart which was set out in the sun. When the blood had dried up hard the hunters would make a hole in the top, wet it with a little hot water and dip in the points of their arrows. But now most of the sheep have been killed off by white men and it is against the game laws to hunt them. The country is becoming so dry that it no longer produces the different kinds of seeds which the Indian women used to gather and the Shoshones have fallen upon hard times.

Their children are sent to Government schools, where they learn the white men's ways; but in these times they find few chances of making money, for the CCC boys do most of the work. T. R. Goodwin, the Superintendent in Charge, reports that, even when he has a job where he could use paid labor, he has difficulty in getting the Indians. They are willing to pack or rent burros, but prefer to stay with the Borax Company jobs, rather than come out and work for the Government.

It is hoped, however, to take them off the Borax Company property, where they have their camp, and establish them in a colony where they can carry on their arts and crafts. The older women are expert basket-makers, weaving baskets of a very fine texture, superior even to those of the Paiutes and only half as thick. Some of the earlier baskets are works of art, showing figures of deer and mountain sheep and eagles, and very beautiful designs of wild-grape leaves and ferns. The characteristic mark is a series of black and white spaces along the rim, generally in sets of three or six.

Under the Death Valley National Monument Administration the Indians are being given trust patents to their springs and the little patches of land which they cultivate, and an effort is being made not to pauperize them or wean them from their old ways. The Shoshones are the highest form of wild life in Death Valley, and the most interesting; but whether they can stay wild and still make a living is a matter of serious doubt. In any case the old days will soon be forgotten, along with those doughty warriors, Panamint Tom and Hungry Bill.

Chapter Five

Borax

For twenty years after the last emigrant left Death Valley, it remained as empty as before. Two parties came back to look for the Lost Gunsight Mine, supposed to have been discovered by Jayhawkers while passing through Emigrant Canyon and reported to be rich in silver. So rich, in fact, that the man who picked up the single specimen had it mounted on his rifle for a gunsight. Then, in 1880, came the discovery of borax and Death Valley's only industry began.

At that time borax was used principally as a drug, bringing about 50¢ a pound, but before the Borax Company got through scraping it up from the marshes it was discovered in lode form at Ryan, in the Funeral Range. After that, production was confined more to the lode deposits and a calcining and concentrating plant was located at Death Valley Junction, which operated for ten or fifteen years, when a better deposit was opened up in the Kramer District. While the mining operations at Ryan have been suspended, the Company still holds its Death Valley properties in order to resume production if necessary.

Borax is now used commercially in making soap and water-softeners, for enamel and glass manufacture and as a glaze for porcelain. During the World War it was used to keep the soldiers from getting "trench feet" and it is said to be the mildest of antiseptics.

The borax deposited at Ryan is from an ancient lake-bed, which has been broken up and lifted by volcanic eruptions. It lies on a sandstone base, where it is overlaid with a black lava capping; and more of it is found in the white hills lower down. The Borax Company has a water supply at Furnace Creek, which has been helpful in its operations. Now that Death Valley has been declared a National Monument the Federal Government has stepped in and the Valley has become a winter play-ground for tourists.

The discovery of borax in Death Valley is credited to Aaron Winters and his wife Rosie, who were living in poverty at Ash Meadows when a strolling prospector came along and told them of the borax mining further north. He stayed over night, still dwelling upon the fortune which awaited any man discovering borax; and from him Winters extracted a chemical test in which, if successful, the mixture would burn green. Then, going over to Death Valley, they camped at Furnace Creek and took a sample of the deposit on the marsh.

The deposit burned green, Winters swore they were rich; and when William T. Coleman, already a borax magnate, sent a man to make him an offer, he sold out for twenty thousand dollars. A few years later Winters discovered the deposit at Amargosa. Then, while Coleman was working his Death Valley claims, a deposit of borate was located in Furnace Creek Canyon by an old Mormon, Philander Lee. Others rushed in to stake claims, but they all sold out to Coleman, who finally went bankrupt and sold out to F. M. Smith, the Borax King.

The romance of borax mining is told at length in a paper-covered book, now out of print, called: *Illustrated Sketches of Death Valley and Other Borax Deserts of The Pacific Coast.** It was written in 1892, by John R. Spears, an experienced newspaper man employed by the *New York Sun,* who described in particular the huge 20-mule teams which have become the sign and symbol of borax. He went through the desert country with a shrewd eye for its inhabitants, recording details of the life of the "white Arabs" which did not go well with the old-timers.

---

* A reprint edition of *Illustrated Sketches of Death Valley* has been published by the Sagebrush Press. Order direct or through your local bookstore.

But he gave a true picture of the country, and especially of the borax industry; and to this I have added the testimony of Frank Tilton, who drove a team for sixteen years. Altogether he has been in the employ of the company for forty-three years; and, in case he might be misinformed, we referred the matter to Wash W. Cahill, now Superintendent of the Tonopah and Tidewater Railroad, who has been with them forty-four years.

According to Mr. Tilton the early teams had only ten mules and the first borax-wagons went to Daggett, on the Santa Fe Railroad. Mr. Cahill, however, says that these were just supply wagons and the big twenty-mule teams went to Mojave. It was a hundred and sixty-five miles, either way, but the road to Mojave was graded and well kept up, and was the route of the famous teams. Tilton's account of the origin of the twenty-mule team is interesting and his picture of the early days is unique.

"I used to be a carpenter and was working on the new sheds of the borax-works at Furnace Creek when I quit and became a swamper on a team. The drivers at that time received four dollars a day and their grub, but a carpenter got only two dollars and a half and paid a dollar and a quarter for his board. My job as swamper was to cook while the driver took care of the mules and to help with the driving of the teams, but at the end of thirty days I had learned my job so well they gave me a new team to handle.

"We used to use ten mules to a team, but on the road to Daggett there was one bad place, where we crossed the boggy Amargosa Sink. It cut the size of our load by half. When we got stuck we would drop the trailer, hook twenty mules on the lead-wagon and pull it through. Then we would go back and bring up the trailer—and so on, with every load. The rest of the road was all right and the Superintendent finally figured out if he used twenty mules all the time we could travel faster and double the load.

"There were two horses for wheelers, six mules up in front

for leaders and twelve more in the middle for pointers. These pointers would jump the chain in pairs when we were going around a curve and pull off to the outside, so that sometimes the wagons would be going one way while the leaders were going the other. The driver sat on the wagon, instead of riding a wheeler as you generally see in the pictures. The Superintendent told us not to ride the wheeler—he had enough to do, already.

"Castor oil was used to grease the wheels. They had a hole bored down through the hub and stopped with a cork. We would pull ahead half a mile to warm up the box, and lots of times we would have to warm up the oil over a fire. Then we would shoot it down the hole with a long, engineer's oil-can. A little—it didn't take much.

"At the fixed camps along the road we would put the mules in a corral, water and feed them and let them roll. At four A.M. they were tied in their stalls and harnessed. After breakfast we led the leaders out first and hooked them on the end of the long chain. Each pair knew its place and would stand there. The wheelers were hooked up last. The driver had a jerk-line to the leaders, a jockey stick between their heads and a buck-line to make it work. The left line of the leaders was short and when the driver pulled it would draw their heads to the left. When he jerked it, they would turn to the right.

"Daggett was headquarters for the borax teams. Twelve miles from Daggett, on the east end of Calico Mountain, was Borate, a regular town. The mine was finally abandoned on account of swelling ground. W. T. Coleman of San Francisco worked three places near Death Valley—Amargosa, Harmony and Eagle Borax. The borax was gathered from the marshes by Chinamen —no white man could stand the job. They had sleds, and a shovel to scoop up the cotton-ball from the trenches. Then they used ropes a hundred feet long to snake the sleds up to the road, where a white man would collect the borax in a two-wheeled cart and haul it to the reduction plant.

Borax

"There it was boiled, using mesquite brush and greasewood for fuel, crystallized in vats and sacked. The brush was hauled in on big wagons, like hay, and Hungry Bill and Panamint Tom took a contract for ten dollars a cord. They would dig away the sand from a half-covered mesquite tree, hook a team on the stump and drag it out. It would have roots on it fifty feet long—they made money at it. Then they took a contract for five hundred dollars to make a road across the salt-bed—what they now call the Devil's Golf Course. They beat the frozen waves flat with sledge-hammers and made another clean-up.

"When Searles Lake was opened up for potash the Borax Company sunk a well a thousand feet deep, right out there by that salt-pool, but all they found was rocks and more salt. While Coleman was hauling borax from Death Valley to the railroad, F. M. Smith was working up north, at Teel's Marsh and Columbus, and making money. The long haul broke Coleman. He couldn't compete, and finally Smith bought him out. He made money from the start.

"Colemanite had been discovered long before, at Ryan and the Lila C., but they could not reduce it and get the borax. The chemists kept trying new processes and tearing them out. When they did find a way the Company abandoned the Death Valley marshes and moved up the mountain to Ryan. And when they got that all fixed up and a railroad put in, somebody bored a deep well on the plains east of Kramer, and they found a better mine yet. So they moved over to Kramer, which is right on the railroad, and abandoned Death Valley to the tourists."

Wash Cahill has another point of view regarding Coleman. He says the long haul had nothing to do with his bankruptcy. He was spread out all over California and Oregon, in the wholesale hardware business and everything else—didn't understand the borax business and couldn't stop to learn it. When Smith got things systematized and a good road laid out, he could haul borax from Death Valley to Mojave for one cent a pound, and it sold by the car-load at around ten.

"Smith divided the road to Mojave into ten sections, driving sixteen miles a day. All the twenty-mule teams went out that way, and each teamster had one lap of the road. On one day he went out loaded, and changed wagons at the station with another man coming in. The next day he turned back with the half-empty wagons, and that gave his mules a rest. They kept ten teams going and as every driver knew his own section of the road best it made it better, all around.

"As for Smith, with a relay of teams along the road from Daggett, he would drive the whole distance, one hundred and sixty-five miles, in one day. He was a great organizer and made lots of money, until he stepped out of his specialty. When he took over the Key Route Railroad, and other interests, it broke him."

The story of the twenty-mule teams is given at some length by Spears. For the first year the borax was freighted from Death Valley by Charles Bennett, but when his contract expired the Company set out to do the hauling itself. The details of this plan were left to J. W. S. Perry, later Superintendent of the Borate mines near Daggett, and it was he who designed the enormous wagons which became almost as famous as the teams and may still be seen standing in the desert sun, strong and solid after sixty years.

The hind wheel was seven feet in diameter. Its tire was eight inches wide and one inch thick. The hubs were eighteen inches in diameter and twenty-two inches long. The wagon-beds were sixteen feet long, four feet wide and six feet deep, and each wagon weighed nearly four tons. Two of these wagons would carry forty-five thousand pounds of borax, exclusive of water and feed for men and teams—the capacity of an ordinary freight car. All ten of them were in use, on one of the worst deserts in America, for a period of five years, without a single breakdown.

Borax

Altogether it was a wonderful achievement in wagon-building, and they were all constructed in Mojave by days' work at a cost of nine hundred dollars apiece. Meanwhile the road had been graded, the three springs along the line developed, and ten stations established where the men and teams could be cared for. Each outfit consisted of two wagons and a water-tank on wheels, and it required only two men to run it.

The human imagination can hardly conceive of the precision with which these outfits worked. The teams went out to Death Valley, got loaded, and returned to Mojave on the twentieth day—at three o'clock. They travelled back and forth like a shuttle, in the terrible heat of summer and over roads often swept by cloudburst. Now all we have to remember them by is the old wagons, still standing, with advertisements of borax on their sides.

Chapter Six

The Lost Breyfogle Mine

The Death Valley country, being volcanic and therefore highly mineralized, has attracted hundreds of prospectors; but, just because it is so broken and shattered, it runs more to gash-veins and surface outcroppings than to large ore-bodies and fissure-veins. It has had many rich strikes and mining excitements, without showing very many veins that widened out and improved with depth.

Yet the very name of Death Valley suggests gold and hidden treasure and, even in this age where the Ford has taken the place of the burro, men are still prospecting its mountains for gold. The Jayhawkers, though they were fleeing for their lives, were not too busy to start the first excitement—the search for the Lost Gunsight Mine. In 1862, Manly himself went back to look for it, and in 1864 Darwin French led a party which discovered, instead of the Gunsight, the old Antimony Mine, above Wild Rose.

But the first prospector to set the world afire was Louis Jacob Breyfogle, in 1864. The story of his lost mine, which is still being sought, has already passed into the Age of Fable. Some say he was going south—others say he was going north. Some say he was following two other men—others say they were following him. But all agree that, when picked up half-crazy on the old Mormon Trail, he had samples of reddish-brown quartz that were over half gold.

The commonly accepted story twenty years ago, before the

more fantastic variations were added, is as follows—told to me by Smitty, a burro-man from Rhyolite, when we came to Daylight Spring.

"This spring was called Daylight by a man named Breyfogle who was taken prisoner by the Indians in the early days. While coming down Death Valley on a prospecting trip his horses were stolen in the night and his two pardners were killed. Breyfogle was a very big man and the Indians rode him like a mule, using him for a beast of burden.

"They kept him up on a mountain-top—probably the Panamints—where there were pines, and from which he could look down into a white valley with three green spots in it. He found some very rich ore and escaped with it during the night, travelling east and reaching Daylight Spring at daylight. He made his way back to Austin with the specimens, and several expeditions set out with him to find the mine, but every time he approached the scene of his suffering he became crazy and could not find it.

"Prospectors are still searching for the Breyfogle Mine. It is somewhere in the Funeral Range, probably overlooking Death Valley. Surveyors' Well, Salt Creek and Cow Creek would be the three green spots which he could see in the white land below. The water in the Funeral Mountains always occurs in a limestone formation, which leaves a white mark on the mountain-side; so prospectors in search of water always look around for white spots. At Cow Creek the water comes out along several hundred yards of white rock, making a heavy growth of mesquite trees and willows."

Herman Jones, of Shoshone, is as much of a specialist on the Lost Breyfogle Mine as he is an authority on Burnt Wagons. He got most of his information from Old Man Finley, who was a member of the original party of ten which took Breyfogle back to Death Valley, after he recovered from his long illness in Austin. But Jones thinks the lost mine lies far to the south of Daylight Spring, only a short distance from Shoshone, and defends his theory as follows:

"Breyfogle was one of the first prospectors to pass through Death Valley. He came down from the north alone, but was followed by two men who thought he was going to a mine. They caught up with him at Furnace Creek and he convinced them that he had no mine. They turned back and he kept going, and somewhere between there and Stump Spring, where he was picked up, he must have found his mine.

"At Furnace Creek he had no gold with him—otherwise the two men would have stayed with him. Somewhere south of there he found some reddish-brown quartz, decomposed on one side, that was over half gold; but, when he was found at Stump Spring with the samples, he had been hit over the head and was nutty. He couldn't tell where he found it, but in his saner moments he kept repeating that it was near a place where two canyons came together, forming a spring where there was one big mesquite tree. This answers perfectly to Sheep Head Spring, on the east side of Death Valley, and near there I believe it will be found.

"I know that Breyfogle went out that way because a Paiute Indian named John Scott told me. We were going out past Bradbury Spring when Scott pointed to the ridge above and said that was where Breyfogle had gone. He was travelling on the ridges, going east and looking for the Colorado River—probably expecting every time he looked over a divide to see the river ahead. The fact that John knew this proves that the Shoshones from Furnace Creek had followed Breyfogle. They know his trail this far, but when he passed east into the Paiute country of course they had to go back.

"Ash Meadows Charley, the old war-chief of the Paiutes, admitted to me that he was with the party which followed Breyfogle's enormous footprints until they came up with him at Stump Spring, near Resting Spring. While Breyfogle was leaning over cooking, one of the Paiutes hit him on the back of the head with a warclub and knocked him out. They took his big shoes and his food and left him for dead, but he recovered and headed north along an old Indian trail which later became the stage road. It was travelled by Fremont and Carson when they came west and was called the Old Spanish Trail.

"Breyfogle was crazy most of the way home; but he held onto his gold—which the Indians had left, not knowing that it had any value. Breyfogle was sick at Austin, Nevada, for over a year. Then Finley and the rest of the ten men took him back to Death Valley. But they found he was too crazy to locate the place, so went ahead prospecting on their own account. Finley was in the Death Valley country many years and I got to know him well, but we never found the mine."

From one authority we turn to another, in the person of R. J. or "Dad" Fairbanks. He holds to the story which is generally believed, that Breyfogle travelled east up Boundary Canyon—past the two or three black buttes named Death Valley Buttes on the maps, but more often called the Breyfogle Buttes. He got to Daylight Spring at daylight and turned southeast: and, west of Eagle Mountain, below Death Valley Junction, Ash Meadows Charley and his warriors cut the trail of his huge "moccasins."

These were the shoes which Breyfogle is reputed to have used to carry water with when passing over the desert stretches —huge brogans with nail-studded soles. The Indians could not believe that the man lived who could throw such an enormous track and, largely out of curiosity, they trailed him to Resting Spring. There they robbed and left him, but he was found by a passing party of Mormons, who took him north.

Another authority on the Breyfogle Mine is A. K. Ishmael of Death Valley Junction. He claims he came to the country six years before Dad Fairbanks and is the oldest old-timer of them all. He has a different story to tell, in which Breyfogle is travelling the other way.

"Breyfogle followed two men from Austin, thinking they were going to some mine. At Daylight Springs, which they came to when heading west, they stopped and asked him what he wanted. When he told them his belief that they were going to some mine they assured him he was wrong. They were just two Southerners, who were going by a round-about way to join the Confederate Army—first to California, then down to Mexico and east across the country till they crossed the Rio Grande into Texas.

"From Daylight Spring, Breyfogle could look to the west and see the Death Valley marshes but he thought they were the Colorado River. He went home with some rich ore and came down a second time with a party of men from Austin. They stopped at Cow Creek and told him they would kill him unless he showed them where his mine was, but he got away and returned to Austin with more of the identical ore.

"On a third trip he lost his horses, climbed a peak where he could see the Breyfogle Buttes and turned back to the east. Going south across the desert he was clubbed by some Paiute Indians and went crazy. I got this dope straight from Pony Duncan and old Man Matson, who were hunting for the Breyfogle in this country in the very early days.

"The early emigrants discovered a mine at the south-east corner of Tucki Mountain which might very easily have been the Breyfogle but more likely was the Gunsight. I found an old anvil there and a big boulder of galena which they probably took for silver. Also there was some very rich gold. I located the claim and sunk a shaft fifty feet, but when I went back a cloudburst had filled the shaft and covered up all trace of the mine."

This last is also the opinion of Death Valley Scotty. After searching for the Breyfogle for years he finally came to the conclusion that it had been swept away by a flood or buried by cloudbursts. A specimen of the original Breyfogle ore is said to be on exhibition at the courthouse in Austin, Nevada. It is decomposed quartz, of a reddish-brown color, and simply rotten with gold.

Several rich mines have been positively identified as the

Lost Breyfogle. The Bullfrog Mine, and the First National at Rhyolite, are both in sight from Daylight Spring, from which place Breyfogle claimed he could see his mine; and the ore of the famous Jumbo at Goldfield is said to be the same reddish-brown quartz.

Even the Indians of Death Valley have heard about the Lost Breyfogle Mine, but any killings that have taken place during the search for it they blame on their enemies, the Paiutes. Tom Wilson tells the story:

"In the early days, over in Kern County, the white people were fighting the Paiutes near South Fork, and some Paiutes came into the Panamints to get away. In the winter time these Paiutes were camped at Furnace Creek when four white men came, asking for gold rock. The Paiutes told them—over at Breyfogle Buttes.

"The Paiutes took two of the white men over there and killed them. Indian George saw them get killed, but he was not in on it. The Paiutes came back and tried to kill the other two white men, but they had guns and got away. They went back to Independence—there was a fort there, with soldiers.

"The two white men came back the next week with soldiers. They came down Cottonwood Canyon, but there was nobody in Death Valley. The Indians were all in the mountains. The Shoshones buried one of the two men that had been killed. He had a ring on his hand, but they buried that with him. They could not get it off. Then the Shoshones got mad at the Paiutes and told them to go back where they came from. So the Paiutes left. I asked a white man named Duncan what kind of rock the Breyfogle Mine had and he said: 'Like a brick. It was kind of red, I guess.' "

Well, neither Indians nor white people have been able to find that brown quartz, though all of them have their theory about where the gold should be found. Most of them look near the Breyfogle Buttes or within sight of Daylight Springs—and certainly several rich mines have been discovered in that area.

The Lost Breyfogle Mine

There was the Keane Wonder and Chloride Cliff, very close; and, further away, Bullfrog and the famous Montgomery-Shoshone, which turned out millions in gold. These were rich, but the Breyfogle was richer—and so they press on, still trying to follow the trail of that huge, tireless prospector with a crazy look in his eye.

This is the story as we get it in Death Valley; but the name Breyfogle is a very unusual one so a search was made for it in the telephone directories of thirty-seven cities, only five of which contained it at all. The first letter written to one of these addresses revealed a relative of the original Breyfogle, William R. Breyfogle of San Francisco, who explained the origin of the name.

"The Breyfogle Family originally came from Berlin, Germany, on one of the first vessels from that country, arriving about the time of the *Mayflower*. They settled in Pennsylvania and had the spelling of their name changed from Breivogel to Breyfogle. They wished to be recognized as Americans, I think. Jacob's Grandfather (my great-grandfather) lived to be over a hundred. He was born, lived and died in the same house in Pennsylvania and had fourteen sons. He attended to all his business affairs up to within a very short time of his death.

"In regard to the name of Mr. Breyfogle, the old miner, I think it was Louis Jacob, but could not be positive, it is so long since my father told me about him. My father, William O. Breyfogle, and this cousin came across the plains from Ohio together with an Ox-train in the early fifties. They landed in Portland, Oregon, and walked to San Francisco. In a few years my father went into the lumber business. His cousin got the gold fever and my father staked him. In 1864 he found this mine in Death Valley. He brought back a large specimen of solid gold. Father told me it weighed eighteen ounces.

"I was born in San Francisco, July sixth, 1868, and Mother told me of her giving him money to go on his last journey— in 1868, after my birth. He returned to Salt Lake City and took a crew of men and started out with them equipped to develop the mine. After getting into the Valley they lost their bearings and his crew deserted him—but he continued on for several days and finally found the spring which gave him his bearings and he finally found his mine again. He returned to the spring to camp for the night. He was surrounded by Indians and was shot by them with a poisoned arrow.

"The Indians disappeared, leaving him to die. After they had gone he managed to get on his mule and started back to Salt Lake City. A few days after he got back to Salt Lake he died of blood-poisoning. Though he had the best of medical treatment it was of no avail.

"He left a map of the claim with my Father, so Father could carry on in case anything should happen to him. Father let another cousin have the map as they were going to try to relocate the claim, but he died and after his death we could not find the map.

"This is a brief outline of the facts as my Father told me and are the true facts as told me by both my Father and my Mother. My father never mentioned anything about him having been captured and held by Indians. The facts as I have told you were written to my Father by Jacob's wife, from their home in Salt Lake City where she and Jacob lived. He may have had some assistance from some Mormons in getting back to his home, as he was undoubtedly quite ill before he reached there."

This authentic information, coming from a member of the Breyfogle family, proves one thing for certain. There was a Breyfogle Mine and it was rich with gold—eighteen ounces in one chunk. So many strange stories have been told about this mine that many people have doubted its existence.

It also establishes the fact that Jacob Breyfogle discovered it in 1864 and returned to it the last time in 1868, the year of his death. As he was beaten over the head with a warclub in 1864, sick a year and returned in 1865 with a party, bringing home some more of the gold, he must have gone to the mine three separate times before an Indian arrow killed him. The fact that the San Francisco branch of the family never heard of his being taken prisoner, or of his being clubbed on the first trip, is easily explained, as they received their information from Jacob's wife. She naturally would suppress that part of the story, and that her husband was considered insane.

Perhaps he was not so crazy after all, for he was able to return twice to his mine and in a country where nearly everybody gets lost. The story of his death from a poisoned Indian arrow will be news to the treasure-seekers of Death Valley, and if he came from Salt Lake City instead of Austin, they will have to revise some of their theories. If he came and went by way of Austin, and recruited his party there, then the old-timers are correct when they claim he entered Death Valley from the north. But, since he went out both times by way of Resting Spring and the Old Spanish Trail, that would argue that he entered from the south.

All we know then is that there *is* a Lost Breyfogle Mine, that it is within a short distance of a spring, and that at that spring the Indians shot him with a poisoned arrow. If that is the case, and the Indians have been keeping it dark, they must know where the spring is. Perhaps they know where the mine is. But can the white men make them admit it, and lead them to the spot? And if, in some forgotten trunk, the Breyfogles can locate that *map,* perhaps the lost mine will be found.

Chapter Seven

Old Panamint

Panamint is a name to conjure with, having been used with great success by several Western writers who have never seen the place. It lies, not in a barren, sunstruck desert but up a deep canyon in a beautiful valley, with water and grass and trees. The mines were discovered in 1873 by a band of stage-robbers who had fled across Death Valley from Nevada, taking refuge above the gorge of Surprise Canyon, which effectually turned back the officers. It is almost at the summit of the Panamint Mountains, but on the western side of the peaks.

Having found these rich deposits of silver the outlaws, according to the local story, sent samples of the ore to Senator Stewart, a very able lawyer, and offered to sell him their claims for twenty thousand dollars if he would square them with the Wells-Fargo Express Company, whose treasure-boxes and passengers they had robbed. The Senator, in his *Reminiscences,* treats the matter rather facetiously; but the deal was made in some form or other—he prefers to call it a "purchase."

But as the stage-robbers, after completing the transaction, stepped out of a San Francisco bank they were arrested and sent to Nevada, where they were convicted and sent to the penitentiary. Not long afterward, however, their attorney effected their release and they returned to enjoy their new freedom in Panamint, where they had lots of other outlaws for company. Two of the original stage-robbers lived to a ripe old age at Panamint and Ballarat, where they were honored and respected members of the community, and actively engaged in mining.

W. A. Chalfant, in his carefully documented *The Story of Inyo* gives quite another account of this transaction.

"Senator Jones and Stewart had paid three hundred and fifty thousand dollars for some of the more prominent claims. Many other sales were made. Some of the early locaters bore unsavory reputations, and perforce had to do business through trusted middlemen. In one instance, a sale was made and the owners went to San Francisco to get their money. At this juncture representatives of Wells-Fargo and Company stepped in and demanded twelve thousand dollars to cover losses due to former depredations on the express company's treasure box by some of the parties who were selling the mines. The party chiefly concerned was given his choice of making that payment or submitting to arrest. He paid and coolly asked for a receipt in full."

A great deal of money was spent in building a long road across the desert to the railroad, and many companies were formed in Los Angeles and other places to develop Panamint mines. Some of the ore ran four thousand dollars to the ton and when it was exhibited by stock promoters the boom began in earnest.

After buying up the principal claims Senators Jones and Stewart put men to work prospecting two mines, the Wyoming and the Hemlock. They sank two shafts between well-defined walls and, finding ore that averaged two or three hundred dollars a ton, erected a very expensive mill and reduction works. Then it was that the leader of the outlaws, who had been lingering about the camp, came to Senator Stewart and asked him when he expected to begin shipping the bullion.

The mill was running, they were getting out plenty of ore, when it came over them suddenly that this gang of ex-stage-robbers were just waiting to steal their treasure. Being too lazy to work the mines themselves they had sold them with the expectation of making a clean-up at the end. Senator Stewart went to the Wells-Fargo Express Company, which was in the business of handling silver and gold, but for once the company declined to accept a shipment and Stewart saw he would have to guard it himself.

He finally solved the problem by making moulds so large that a ball of solid silver could be cast, weighing seven hundred and fifty pounds. Then they began the final reduction of their ore, running off cannon-balls of silver so big they could have been used to bombard a battleship. When the road-agents saw these they acted as if they had been cheated and remonstrated with Mr. Stewart, but he sent out the treasure on their regular freight wagons, without a guard of any kind. Since there was only one road across the desert to the railroad the shipments could not be diverted, and there was no way of breaking up the cannon-balls or reducing them to a smaller size.

The outlaws were stumped and for a time all went well, but as they worked the mines they found that in both cases the apparent veins were only "pipes" and did not extend to any depth. Out of these "pipes" and the ore on the surface the mining company claims to have extracted about a million dollars, but the Senator admits that "the abrupt termination of the ore involved a large loss to the investors."

This "abrupt termination" was caused, however, not by the petering out of the ore deposit, but by a terrific cloudburst which swept down Surprise Canyon and cut off the camp in a day. The eight miles of road, which had been built at great expense, was absolutely destroyed and the inhabitants went out over the ridges, leaving everything just as it was. For many years afterward, according to all the old-timers around Ballarat, the glasses could be seen still stacked up before the mirror in the bar of the big saloon.

For many years after the cloudburst the sole inhabitant of Panamint was a crazy Dutchman called Radiator Bill, because of his belief that the entire mountain was composed of radium. But the ground was not worked out and one by one the old claims were relocated or simply "chlorided" for picked ore by old miners. Two of the most determined of these were Judge Curran and Jack Byrne; and for eighteen years, while they were packing their ore out on burros, they labored to reconstruct the road which the cloudburst had so completely destroyed.

The job was completed in August, 1918, with the aid of S. F. Hopkins and Harry Wellman; but the summer heat was so intense in the shut-in canyon that they were compelled to await cooler weather. Tons of rich ore were lying on the dumps, sacked and ready to be shipped, but the radiators of the trucks would boil until they could not pull up the steep road. Six weeks after they had finished it another cloudburst came and tore out the last vestige of the grade.

The miners were at their cabin at the mouth of Surprise Canyon when, over the summits of the Panamints, two cones of white clouds began to gather. They approached each other obliquely, giving off flashes of lightning, exchanging bolts of electricity across the narrowing space until they came together. There was a blaze of white light, a sudden blackening of the mass and the writhing funnel of a waterspout reached down until it touched the earth.

Where it struck the miners did not know, for the mountain walls cut off their view. Two prospectors, camped far up the canyon, heard a rumble which turned into a roar, and ran straight up the slope. Then a mass of brush and tree-trunks came rushing towards them, half hiding the muddy water which banked up behind it, and swept irresistibly on.

The column of falling water had landed in Woodpecker Canyon, millions of tons in one place, and stripped it down to bed-rock. When the flood poured into the main canyon below Panamint City it piled up such a burden of pinyon trees and underbrush that it dammed it and formed a huge lake. The dam broke—the flood swept on down Surprise Canyon until it came to Corkscrew Gorge, just above the miners' cabin. There it formed such a barricade that they could feel the earth tremble as the water and whirling logs fought for mastery.

It overflowed, hurling tree-trunks high into the air, and burst through to form another lake, inundating their little ranch with mud. When the lower dam broke, their orchard had been buried beneath a mixture of gravel and silt which hardened like cement. The road they had toiled on for eighteen years was blotted out of existence—and they were left with their sacks of picked ore still lying on the dump at Panamint. But six weeks later they were back on the job, pecking out a little burro trail to bring down their picked ore, buy some grub and start all over again.

This is a story not given in the books, a record of human fortitude hard to believe; a tribute to the stout hearts of Western pioneers, the last chapter in the history of Panamint.

Chapter Eight

Smitty

Henry L. Smith, called "Smitty," was a prospector of the old school and a burro-man second to none. Though he cursed them and hurled clubs at them to make them go, his whole being was wrapped up in the five burros of his pack-train and in Pal, the little dog that travelled with them. He really loved them all and was ready to fight for them, as I learned when we first got acquainted.

It was in Rhyolite in 1916, ten years after the boom had broken, leaving a city that had once housed ten thousand for the desert-rats to move into. There were about forty people left, mostly old-time miners still clinging to their claims and living on faith, hope and charity. They spent their days in the barroom of the hotel, playing pinochle and stud-poker for the drinks and hoping some "live one" would come through.

I had been there four days—waiting for an automobile which never came, to show me through Death Valley in style—when, from my room above the bar, I heard a terrible outburst of cursing. Two men, both hollering at once and threatening death and destruction. It sounded as if a shooting was about to take place, but as usual it was only talk. Then one of them stopped for breath and I found out what it was all about.

"You keep them burros away from my mine or I'll shoot 'em, so help me God!"

"You shoot them burros and I'll shoot *you!*"

This last came from Smitty, and it sounded as if he meant

it. The man who was going to shoot his beloved burros was a care-taker engaged to "herd" the Montgomery-Shoshone Mine, which had once turned out millions in gold. After the tumult and the shouting had died down I ventured into the bar and found Smitty almost in tears.

He was a little man with his nose laid over on one side and the fire of a great anger in his eyes. It was the care-taker who was drunk—he was drunk all the time—and Al Meyers, the proprietor, had shushed him down and was edging Smitty outside. I followed along and listened while he told the world at large what he would do to the so-and-so who raised a hand against his burros.

That took some time and, being tired of waiting for the auto, it occurred to me that Hank might be a good man to take me into Death Valley. A pack-train looks fine in a desert picture, and Smitty could tell me some good stories. So I brought up the subject of a trip and was just about to close the deal with him when Al Meyers beckoned me inside.

"Don't go out with that fool," he said. "He's crazy, and the dirtiest yap in town. You couldn't eat his grub, I know."

Well, all burro-men are crazy, as far as that goes; and I could do the cooking myself. So I hired him for five dollars a day and found, and he went out to round up his burros. He found them right away, which was a good sign, showing that he treated them well; and we put them in a corral over night, so they wouldn't get wise and pull out.

Smitty sported a good outfit, having had the pick of all the abandoned pack-boxes and saddles within a hundred miles; and we had one burro loaded with nothing but water, for the Death Valley water-holes are bad. He had picked up at some abandoned mine two pack-boxes equipped with separate two-gallon cans, which when full, would eliminate the "slosh" of half-empty oil-cans. We had lots of grub, our beds, a bucket and a short-handled shovel. Prospectors don't carry picks on their burros except in the illustrated magazines. All they have is a short-handled prospector's pick stuffed in some pack-box.

From Rhyolite the road runs absolutely straight for ten miles, across the plain to Daylight Spring, where Breyfogle stopped for a drink. Then down the canyon for six miles more, when we came to Hole-In-The-Rock Spring. There was a corrugated iron house there then, built for the use of freighters, but not a stick of wood as far as the eye could see. I gathered some desert holly in the slack of a rope while Smitty watered the burros.

The spring is two hundred yards away, up a side canyon, marked by the word WATER stamped in holes through a metal sign. The hole is a foot and a half across, and it is two feet down to the water so animals have to kneel to drink, unless the water is dipped up for them. For this purpose a bucket is always left at the spring, with a shovel to dig out the sand, and for a man to steal them or knock down the sign would be considered a capital crime.

It was December, and a cold wind was blowing in from the north. Smitty opened a few cans, threw down a greasy canvas and cooked over a very small fire. Then he got out the dirty dishes I had heard so much about and told me to go to it. The old tin plates were rusty and battered, but there was one as clean and white as you could wish and as I sat down I picked it up.

"No, no!" protested Smitty, "you can't have that plate. It belongs to Pal."

I gave Pal her plate, with apologies, and started to dip out some white corn-meal mush which he had prepared with especial care. But that, it seems, had been cooked for Pal too, and she ate it out of the clean plate. But she was a nice little dog and in a delicate condition anyway as she was expecting her puppies within a month, so I compromised by taking a tin plate and filling up on bacon and canned corn. Then she crawled back under Smitty's warm blankets and we turned in to get out of the cold.

All day, as we headed west out of Rhyolite, Smitty had trudged along in silence. He was an economical tobacco-chewer and there was no use trying to talk with him on the trail. It hurt his feelings to have to waste a whole chew of tobacco every time I asked a question, so I waited until he had to spit in order to curse out his burros. Every time one of them lagged behind he would grab up a rock or rush at him with his club, and Pal would charge in, barking.

Then, having stood in with her master and been kicked at by the burro, she would turn around and bark at Smitty. This, Hank explained, was to intercede for the burros; and, very obligingly, he would desist. He said she would stand in with the burros against him, every time. Little Pal was the brains of the outfit and she figured she was running everything. Every time we passed over rough ground she would take a run and leap up on old Jinny's pack, but her real friend among the burros was Johnny.

He was young, dark and handsome; and that night at Stove Pipe Hole Smitty told me all about it. He could talk all day about his burros. Johnny was a camp-robber and when his master would go out prospecting, he would try to get his head inside the tent. But it was Pal's job to guard that tent, and toward all the other burros she was adamant. She would bark at them and bite them—all but Johnny.

Several times Smitty had looked down when returning to camp and caught Johnny stealing his grub—and Pal, sitting beside him and wagging her tail. It made all the other burros mad. But when Pal saw her master coming home one day while Johnny had his head in the tent, she flew at the burro and bit him. Not knowing what it was all about, Johnny kicked out and struck her, and when Smitty rushed down and beat him he ran away and was gone for two days.

Every summer Smitty went to his little mine north of Saline Valley and ground out gold with what he called his "rasper." It was a Mexican *arrastre,* about fifteen feet across and built

Borax Marsh in Death Valley.
(Photograph by Dane Coolidge)

PANAMINT CITY.

Discovered by Stage Robbers in 1873. Cut off from the World by a Waterspout which destroyed the road down Surprise Canyon.

(Photograph by Dane Coolidge)

SMITTY, JOHNNY AND LITTLE PAL AT HOLE-IN-THE-ROCK SPRING.

(*Photograph by Dane Coolidge*)

Drifting Mountains of Sand That Turned Back the Forty-Niners.

(Photograph by Dane Coolidge)

(Photograph by Dane Coolidge)

OSCAR DENTON

Who stayed through the heat eight summers at Furnace Creek.

Dayton's Grave in 1916.

Surrounded by the bones of his horses which perished with him.

(Photograph by Dane Coolidge)

© D.C.

THE HAPPY FAMILY IN DEATH VALLEY.
Pal riding on Jinny and barking at Baby. Smitty behind, with his club.
(*Photograph by Dane Coolidge*)

JOHN LEMOIGNE OF COTTONWOOD CANYON
panning for gold. He held his mine for a quarter of a million dollars for over forty years, then perished in Death Valley from the heat.

(Photograph by Dane Coolidge)

on a concrete foundation, in which was embedded in a circle, uneven blocks of stone. A big stone was then attached to a sweep and dragged round and round over the ore by a burro on the other end.

In the cracks between the foundation stones a little quick-silver was placed to catch the gold, then some ore was thrown in, drenched with water, and the weary drag began. The burro was blindfolded and belled and started on his rounds, while Smitty settled down under a shady bower to sleep or read the magazines. Whenever the bell stopped ringing it would wake Smitty up, and he would yell at the burro and go to sleep again. The ore was dug out of a rich but narrow vein, and packed over two high ridges to the water, where his "rasper" would do the rest. It was Smitty's idea of the ideal life, and maybe he was right.

As we came down from Hole-In-The-Rock that morning we emerged into the Great Valley at Black Point, where six years before Pete Busch had died from the heat. It was on August 7th, 1910, when the highest temperature ever known was recorded at Furnace Creek Ranch—134 degrees.* Pete had started by automobile from Los Angeles and had been warned at Ballarat not to cross Death Valley in the heat. But his brother was waiting for him at the Keane Wonder Mine and he kept on through the night.

His automobile got stalled on the corduroy road that wound through the Devil's Playground and the man who was with him turned back. But Busch took a canteen of water and went ahead. He was found by his brother the next morning, dead, but with water still left in his canteen. It was the heat that had killed him. Smitty says it comes in waves, like wind, from the depths of Death Valley and makes a man so uncomfortable he can neither stop nor rest. Sometimes he digs holes in the sand to get under the heated surface, but generally he presses on and either reaches the mountains or dies.

---

* Official records show that the 134° temperature was made on July 10, 1913.

It is a tragic spot, this Black Point, and some devotee of the new nomenclature has renamed it Hell's Gate. There for the first time I gazed out over the vastness of Death Valley, standing on the place where a man had found his brother dead. And I knew that man, too. I had tried to hire him to drive me down into Death Valley, but he had always put me off. He would have to go past the place where Pete had died—that was why his price was so high. Many times since I have gazed out over the Valley, the silvery marshes under their mist of heat, the long fans of boulders swept down by countless cloudbursts, but it has never looked the same. That first time I was almost afraid.

In the winter time the Valley is swept by cold winds, or sleeps peacefully through long days of calm. It is never really hot and never really dangerous as long as you carry a canteen. But when we arrived at Stove Pipe Hole there was two inches of black scum on top of the water, and a drink of it would kill a mule. There was a grave near by where a hobo miner had been buried. He had taken a big drink without baling out the hole and they found him where he had folded up his coat for a pillow and laid down in the old bottle-house.

First Smitty baled out, then he scraped off the slime, let it fill up and baled it out again; but the burros were accustomed to the sweet water of Rhyolite and they barely drained the bucket. Valley-bred horses would not drink it at all; or, if they did, it made them sick. Smitty's burros had been born and raised in Death Valley; and Pal had been born there, too. Her mother had been a burro-dog before her.

That night they grazed on the wiry salt-grass and the next morning they were all there. I think it was the affection they had for Pal that kept them from pulling out. Stove Pipe Hole was not a very attractive place to camp; but anyhow, we had wood. In the height of its glory the citizens of Skidoo had built a telephone line across Death Valley to Rhyolite, and now both towns were dead. Some daring soul had cut down the first pole, and so it went until Smitty had to hike a quarter of a mile to find one he could drag in. Like most desert prospectors he was a bandit at heart, always jumping mines when the assessment work ran out and stealing all the copper plate and tools.

But no one had camped at the Hole for months and there was no law of man or God. Something about the place seemed to rouse my guide from his apathy and that night by the fire he talked about the wild life he had led. The high spot in it all was when he landed in Guatemala City with his pockets full of American gold and the exchange was two hundred and fifty to one. One good American dollar was worth two hundred and fifty *pesos,* and the people worked for three *reales* a day.

This called for the drinks, and the beer was only two *pesos* a case. He hired the front room of the best hotel in town and, sitting in the window with a case on either side of him, he drank till he could hold no more. Then he invited everyone who looked as if he could speak English to join him, and still they could not get away with it. There was simply too much of it—and it was grand beer, too.

We took pictures in the morning and, out among the sand-hills where the ground had been swept bare, we found the tracks of the covered wagons that had tried to cross the Valley in 1849. Underneath the drifting mountains of sand there is a level plain of damp ground, and in the bunches of ice-plant that grow there we found the holes of kangaroo rats. Croaking ravens flew down in pairs from the heights, passing close with a sudden rustle of wings while they looked us over with ghoulish eyes. They were just waiting around for somebody to drop dead, so that afternoon we moved.

Perhaps we would have done better to stay where we were; for at Salt Wells, where the emigrants are supposed to have died, the water in the hole was undrinkable. So Smitty decided to keep going down the Valley, and we ended up by getting lost. That is the prerogative of all good desert guides, and of course we had a burro-load of water; but about ten o'clock, when our animals turned out for a patch of salt-grass, we camped for the rest of the night.

It was the darkest darkness I have ever seen, and yet the alkali flats were white. The stars shone clear enough, several million of them, but we could not see the hills a few miles away nor the high peaks that towered above them. We had no idea why the burros had quit the trail until we reached down and felt the grass. As a special reward for not leaving us, Smitty treated them to hot flapjacks the next morning.

That was a model family, Smitty and his brother burros, the only pack outfit I have ever seen where the animals did not run away. And every day he cursed them and threw clubs at them. That is the only way a packer can get any speed out of burros and keep them from lying down under their loads. We headed south the next morning as spritely as ever and soon saw a flock of Nevada sage sparrows, sure sign that water was near.

Not more than a mile further we came to Cow Creek where the water comes out along several hundred yards of limestone, making a heavy growth of mesquite trees. We had been following along the edge of the borax-flats, the surface of which was covered with rounded, crystalline forms of a dirty brown color, and when we came to the first mesquite trees we passed a couple of graves. Then, against the base of the eastern hills, we sighted a house and some corrals, but kept on past them and the abandoned Coleman Borax Works till we arrived at Furnace Creek Ranch.

On account of the good water and grass, this is the burros' paradise in Death Valley, the one place they always head for when they run away. First in the distance we saw the tops of three tall palms, then a grove of cottonwoods on the edge of a mesquite thicket which extended clear down to the salt marsh. Along the banks of the ditch which brought the water down from the hills there was a succession of Indian camps, and when we came in sight we saw them running to warn the Boss.

He lived in an old adobe house on the edge of a wide field of alfalfa, and he met us at the gate with a gun. Greenland Ranch, as it was officially called, was of great strategic importance to the Borax Company, and it was always in danger of being "jumped" so our reception could hardly be described as cordial. I had hardly got started on my long explanation about the automobile that never came when he shut me up with a gesture.

"You may be all right," he said, "but how do I know you are a friend of the Borax Company? You have no letter of identification so I will have to ask you to camp outside of the fence."

He stepped inside and shut the gate and we camped, as directed, outside. Mr. Denton was a man ideally fitted for the job of herding this valuable property—tall, dark, with a deeply-lined face and black eyes that bored right through you. Not that it would have been any great privilege to live in the tumble-down old house. Its double-roof and mud walls were overrun with wood rats, which galloped back and forth all night, and the Superintendent did not seem very sociable.

I discovered later that Smitty had been through there once before and, on account of his drunken conduct, had been warned away from the ranch. But in a desert like Death Valley you cannot drive a man away from water; so, in a high north wind, we camped in the lee of some mesquite trees and Smitty exchanged confidences with the Indians. It seemed that, back in Rhyolite, he sold a little whiskey to the Shoshones, though only to the women. They would take their liquor and go away; but the men when drunk would come back and threaten him unless he gave them more.

As it was a penitentiary offense to sell whiskey to Indians, and there was a fifty-dollar reward to informers, Hank had to be very circumspect. But, being broke, he had not been able to bring a single bottle with him and our visitors soon went away. We kept away from the ranch-house and the short-spoken Mr. Denton; but that evening, carrying a pick-handle for a cane, he came out and sat by our fire. The long loneliness of his life, with no one but Indians to associate with, had overcome his stern aloofness and he turned out to be a very pleasant gentleman.

His father, a retired Colonel in the British Army, had been given the Jacumba Land Grant in Old Mexico for surveying in the province of Tehuantepec and had settled down on it, marrying a Spanish lady. But Oscar had had an unpleasant experience during the Mexican Revolution and he had a special reason for being suspicious of strangers, since there were men who had sworn to kill him. He had retreated, in fact, to the most isolated place in North America, and they could not say they were just going by. If they came to Furnace Creek they intended to kill him, and he was ready to act accordingly.

The first of these experiences Mr. Denton told me himself. He was working a mining lease down in Parral, Chihuahua, when Madero, after capturing Juarez, marched south with twelve thousand men to withstand the attack of Diaz' Army, consisting of thirty thousand trained Federals. He fortified the town and, being short of machine-gun operators, he recruited a number among the English and Canadian miners who had been cut off from the Line.

Having known Denton's father, and the training his son had received as a soldier, Madero suggested he take a machine-gun, but Denton told him there was no honor in such warfare and declined to enlist. Madero then suggested that it would be better if he did so, since otherwise it would be necessary to make the situation interesting for him, as an enemy of the Revolution. Denton replied that, since he put it that way, of course he would serve. So he went out to try the machine-gun.

When they put up a sheet for a target he drew a cross on it at two hundred yards, and Madero would not let him go at any price. Denton's sympathies were not with Madero but, knowing that a Mexican gentleman will practically never violate an agreement to which he has put his signature and *rubrica,* he made him agree to buy the ore he had on the dump and gave him a pass to El Paso, if he would serve the machine-gun for two weeks. So, although he said it pained him to do so, he took his place behind the sandbags and, when the Federals charged, he mowed them down until they were piled up "belly deep." Knowing that it was necessary to do so, he shot very carefully, without becoming excited, and was highly complimented for his work by Madero.

Denton's second experience, and the one which had driven him into hiding, occurred at the ranch of his widowed mother in Lower California, shortly after he had returned from Parral. A party of American filibusters had crossed the Line at Mexicali with the purpose of establishing a "red" republic, but the Governor of Baja California marched across the desert from Ensenada, led them into an ambush and killed most of them with machine-gun fire.

The survivors, led by several fighting Reds, fled west across the Peninsula and arrived more dead than alive within sight of Denton's home. They were thirsty and starving, but they took the wrong method of collecting what they considered the world owed them. Denton was watching from the doorway when the first man came in sight and, seeing a steer by the water, raised his gun and killed it. No matter what their condition, Denton felt that they should have asked for the beef, so he picked up his rifle and shot the man dead—and several others who took up the fight.

He drove them away from Jacumba without even letting them get a drink and when they crossed the Line—only to be jailed for violating the neutrality laws—they took an oath to avenge their wrongs. The full malignancy of their hate was discovered by Death Valley Scotty, during one of the numerous incarcerations in the Los Angeles Jail of which he used to be so proud. At this time he was locked in the same cell with a filibuster named Moseby, son of the famous guerilla leader, General Moseby, of the Confederate Army. Mr. Moseby told Scotty he lived but for one thing—to get out of that jail and kill Denton before any of his pardners beat him to it.

With all this, and probably more, behind him it was no wonder that Denton was shy; but, once he became convinced that my intentions were peaceable, he was very polite indeed to me. Never have I met a closer observer; and, as he had been the official weather observer for six years, staying through the most killing heat, his information was worth writing down.

"Most of the men who die in Death Valley are hobo miners who have been paid off and gone on a drunk and have then started across the Valley. Being already in a weakened condition, they cannot stand the strain. Everyone who has gone through it speaks of the fact that a man can feel himself growing weaker and weaker, and if he becomes sick from drinking bad water he gets frightened and goes out of his head.

"In the year of the rush across Death Valley to Skidoo sixteen men were found who had died from heat while travelling the regular trails; and as a man on foot can cross the marsh anywhere by wading through the mud in the middle, many more died and were never found. As there is now practically no travel across the Valley, not a single death was recorded in 1916.

"A common cause of death is ptomaine poisoning, and to leave canned goods in the container for so much as a minute after opening them has been known to bring on ptomaine. Most hobo miners in going from camp to camp have a pack which looks like their blankets but which in reality is mostly canned goods and coffee, and they often get poisoned by trying to carry food in opened tins.

"A roaring in the head is said to presage the insanity which makes these lost men run wild. Their eyes twitch like wild-fire and their pulse at the throat is very strong and erratic. On the day that I recorded the greatest heat ever registered—134 degrees in the shade—I thought the world was going to come to an end. Swallows in full flight fell to the ground dead, and when I went out to read the thermometer with a wet Turkish towel on my head it was dry before I returned.

"The winter months in Death Valley are bright and sunshiny, but the nights are very cold. When storms come up from the south there is often threatening weather for days, but it is only when the north wind sweeps in after a storm that it really rains, and much of this rainfall is in the form of snow. As a southern storm comes up, the first sign is a stratum of mist which bands the Panamint Mountains about halfway up, on the level of the high land all about, the Valley being below sea-level.

"This develops into cloudy weather over the peaks, then along the slopes and, finally, into a furious dust-storm with a few drops of rain, which are instantly dried up. But when the north wind begins, the dust which it carries with it is first seen pouring over the Funeral Range, to the northeast. Then a great pillar of dust comes down the Valley, often preceded by whirlwinds; so well defined is this dust wall that it is possible to step in and out of the edge of it.

"The warm weather begins in March, when it averages around ninety-five almost every day. In April it runs into the one hundreds and in May the first great heat comes on. In June, July and August it is over one hundred almost every day; but the greatest suffering comes when there is humidity, as the nights do not cool off. In August there are sometimes violent thunderstorms and cloudbursts in the mountains on both sides of the Valley, and great floods come down the washes, carrying everything before them.

"These cloudbursts seem to concentrate on a small area of some mountain slope and dig out a great hole clear down to the bed-rock, which shows white for many miles, giving the effect of having been sluiced out hydraulically. As far as I have observed there is practically no rainfall in the Valley—the average is 3/4 of an inch a year—most of the water falling at higher levels and running down into the Sink. This makes the road down the Valley to the south impassable for months at a time, as the corduroy across the slough was long ago washed out.

"Our life-saver here at the ranch is a big fan with a balance-wheel attached which is run by water power from the steel pipe that leads water down to the house. When anyone arrives in an exhausted condition they are given a bath and placed before this fan, where the spray from the power wheel keeps them cool. In the winter four or five families of Shoshones camp at the ranch where the men are hired to clean the ditches, but when the hot weather comes on they all go up into the high mountains.

"I say to them: 'What do you want to go for? You were born and brought up in this Valley.'

"But the Indians say: 'Yes, but we know more now than our people did. We are not crazy. You can stay if you want to, but we will go.' "

Denton said he suffered more from the cold in winter than from the heat in summer, as he was accustomed to high temperatures, having been born and brought up at Jacumba, in the Imperial Valley.

"I am especially adapted to endure hot weather," he said, "and in summer, when the thermometer gets down around eighty or eighty-two, I have to put on my coat. In the winter I wear two flannel shirts, a sweater and a padded coat and yet I suffer greatly from the cold at night, in spite of a mountain of blankets. People laugh at Scotty for wearing an overcoat all summer in Los Angeles, but when I was summoned inside by the illness of my mother I took a terrible chill in spite of my heavy clothing, and only the friendly aid of a barkeeper kept me from developing pneumonia.

"When men are sent down here in the summer to work they get fainting spells, and if they have been drinking they sometimes die. They also become very quarrelsome and excitable and I am afraid to have them around. Of the four superintendents who preceded me, three died and one went to California. I have lasted three years, but it is a question with me how much longer I can stand it."

Oscar Denton made a record by lasting eight summers. He finally quit in 1921 and went back to Jacumba, where he married and settled down, passing away about 1932. He was a wonderful character, always speaking the most perfect English and having very polished manners; but he was a man quick to anger and in any disagreement he could play a leading hand. We parted in the morning with very real regret, but Smitty was glad to get away.

"Did you see that pick-handle he was carrying?" he asked. "He must be afraid some of these Indians will jump him."

I did not tell Smitty, but the pick-handle had been for little Pal. She had barked at Denton that morning, and if she tried to bite him he intended to brain her. We headed south against a strong wind and, as the canteen was roped on a pack, we travelled the whole 17 miles to Tule Hole without a drink. The burros were so terrorized by Hank's driving, they would not stop.

He had that ability, which seems common to all burro-men, of throwing himself into a frenzy of rage while he chased them and hurled rocks and clubs. Pal would always rush ahead, leaping up at the leader's nose and barking in a similar rage; but the moment her master quieted down she would go back and bark at him. Then Smitty would stop cursing, the burros would slow down, and she would leap up and kiss them on the nose, as if apologizing for trying to bite them.

Ten miles below Furnace Creek we turned off to the southwest in order to cross the Sink, passing over the salt-fields now so happily called the Devil's Golf Course. At first the road, once travelled by twenty-mule teams, passed over the brownish borax crystals; then it entered a great field of broken up salt, which extends many miles up and down the Valley on both sides of the narrow slough.

Down the middle of the salt-marsh there is a water-course which drains the Valley after a storm, but the corduroy road had long ago been washed away and we crossed the slough in the mud. To show how little travel there was at that time, we found the tracks where, the year before, a Ford car had got stuck and turned back. Two years later, when I crossed with Shorty Harris, not a single car had passed and the Ford tracks were as plain as ever.

The rock salt on both sides lies in chunks like frozen waves, standing two feet high and with holes between them, down which the devil is supposed to lose his golf-balls. These salt-crests ring like iron when they are struck and the rough road resounded beneath the burros' feet, causing them to shrink back in terror. After a mile or two of this, the road came out on a smooth flat, covered with a white springy surface which makes it as resilient as rubber.

Tule Hole is a round patch of reeds about ten feet across, from the middle of which good water wells up from some fissure leading down from the heights. A well sunk a few feet away from the tules goes down six feet without striking water, thus indicating that some underground passageway exists which brings it straight from the mountains. A similar spring comes up in the pool at Eagle Borax Works, a mile further on; but the pool itself is poison. It is only by going out on a plank and dipping down where the sweet water boils up that a man can get a good drink.

The country, though covered with mesquite trees, was absolutely deserted and, about a quarter of a mile before we reached the Borax Works, we came to Dayton's Grave. Here Jim Dayton, then Superintendent at Furnace Creek Ranch, had perished in the heat while driving to Daggett for supplies. There was an Indian woman living at the ranch and Dayton, who was not well, had tried to persuade her to let her boy go with him, but she refused.

He had been taken sick the first day out, just before reaching water, and had pulled his team out of the road and died. It was twenty-one days before his body was found, and a little dog he had taken with him was still alive and guarding it from the coyotes. A trail was found where he had been trotting back and forth to water, but the horses had been tied fast to the wagon-wheels and had perished miserably.

Dayton was buried where he was found and later the skulls and bones of his horses were placed in an orderly way about his grave. It was considered a great work of art in Death Valley but was recently obliterated to make room for Shorty Harris, who had expressed a wish to be buried there. Now a monument of granite stones marks the place where they both lie, but it will always be a lonely spot.

On returning to Furnace Creek the next day we met Shorty, then in his prime, having a terrible time trying to get his stubborn burros to travel against the wind. Smitty engaged him in a long conversation and reported that he was probably on a jumping expedition, it being near the first of the year, although Shorty said he was going down to the Carbonate Mine to do some assessment work.

On the first of January every year all mining districts are thrown into a frenzy of excitement, and many claims upon which the work has not been done are jumped by other people. Any tools or machinery which happens to be on the ground become the property of the jumper, who immediately gets a little stake by stripping the copper plates from the mills and selling the tram-cars and tracks.

Smitty's favorite method of procedure is to get on the ground a few days before the first of the year, letting it be understood that he is doing the assessment work for the owner. He drills a few holes, shoots off a little powder and waits around until midnight, January first, when he posts his notices and takes possession. In Nevada and Arizona the law requires that one hundred dollars' worth of discovery work shall be done within ninety days, but the California law gives a man practically two

[77]

years. The result is that all the boom camps on the California side of Death Valley have failed because nobody dug; but in Nevada, when there was a rush, everybody began to sink at once and, if there was anything there, they found it.

Eagle Borax Works was nothing but a vat about thirty feet long, three small tanks and a pile of decomposing sacks of borax. It lies at an altitude of 264 feet below sea-level; and the flat to the east, known as Bad Water, is the lowest spot in America. A few miles further south is Bennett's Well, where the Bennett and Arcane families waited while Manly made his trip to Los Angeles.

The south wind died down and it was bitter cold that night, but Smitty got out a fur overcoat—which he had acquired during the hot weather at Rhyolite, when the owner would have no use for it—and, after thawing out by the fire, we agreed to turn back to Furnace Creek Ranch, before we ran into something worse. A big storm was brewing in the south and the wind was blowing up a sandstorm.

I agreed then to return, but I was rather surprised when I found Smitty emptying the last can of water into the dirt.

"Well, what's the difference?" he yelled. "We'll be in Furnace Crick by night. Want to pack it clear back where it come from?"

That seems to be the philosophy of all Death Valley guides —to throw away their water because it is too heavy to carry and travel all day without a drop. But the burros were so wild we couldn't catch them, anyhow, and it was only eighteen miles. With the wind behind us we made it in jig time and camped outside the fence in the dirt. When Denton came in he was very apologetic and insisted on my coming inside; for it seemed that, during our absence, a big automobile had arrived with orders to show us every courtesy, but they could not cross the slough and so had had to turn back.

But, for a photographer, a pack-train is infinitely more desirable than an automobile, and I slept outside with Smitty. It was a wild night, though, and in the morning our beds were coated deep with dust. The long white line which precedes a storm was stretched along the side of the Panamints, and up on the peaks we could see the gathering clouds that mean snow. Very early we packed and headed for Ryan, where the railroad would take me home.

While still on the flats the dust turned to a sandstorm, and up the canyon the gravel began to fly. Smitty took off his fur coat in order to rock the burros on and as we mounted the rain began to fall. It turned into sleet, then snow; and the wind, which came in gusts, almost stopped us. Up the canyon ahead of us there stood a butte of fine red ochre, and every time a gust hit that hill it snatched away a cloud of dust. It did not seem possible for our burros to pass through it, but just as we approached the wind died down, and just as we got past it returned with such fury that it painted the heavens red.

It was a blustering farewell to Death Valley and when we reached Ryan, far up in the Funeral Mountains, the black peaks were white with snow. Poor Smitty was so frozen his hands could hardly hold a stone, but he put his burros through and we camped by the corrals, where we gave them a feed of grain. But they, hardy creatures, disdained the strange food and turned their rumps to the storm.

When train-time came I parted with Smitty and little Pal, and as it happened it was our last farewell. That summer Smitty was killed in a boiler explosion and his happy family broken up. Someone else might have taken over the burros— and even Pal—but it would never be the same for them without Smitty to curse them along.

Chapter Nine

John Lemoigne

John Lemoigne was quite a different type of man from the ordinary burro-cursing prospector. He was calm, polite, philosophical; with polished manners, a ready smile and all the ways of a gentleman. He was a Frenchman—some said a Breton —and a fine figure of a man. Tall, white-bearded, with a clear, ruddy skin and eyes a soft, velvety black. They must have played havoc with more than one feminine heart when he was young and in his prime. Perhaps that is why he came to the Death Valley country and remained there until he died.

He was a wonderful cook and made everybody welcome, and the fame of his coffee spread so far that the lady who ran the restaurant at Keeler fairly begged him to give her the recipe.

"Well, Madame," he said, "it is very simple. You put in a very little water and a great deal of coffee. That is the secret."

We pass on his secret to other harassed keepers of restaurants, where people want the best of everything for twenty-five cents.

When Lemoigne first came into the country, along in the 1870's, he worked underground in the mines around Darwin until he made a stake. Then he bought a grubstake and some burros and began to look for a mine of his own. He must have found it very soon for, for over forty years he lived in Cottonwood Canyon, in the Panamint Mountains, and held it until he died. His price was a quarter of a million dollars, cash, and he did not care whether he sold it or not.

Like his way of making coffee, his way of making a living

was very simple. He did assessment work for neighboring mine-owners at the standard rate of five dollars a day. Twenty days' work, under the law, will hold a mine for a year; and Old John could always be depended upon to sink his full twenty feet. Then he took the hundred dollars, bought his winter's grub, and went back to work on his claim.

It was a silver-and-lead property—a large body of low-grade ore, on the ridge south of Cottonwood Canyon. Nearer the railroad it might have been worth a million, but to the west three high mountains and three desert valleys lay between it and the tracks at Keeler; and to the east there was Death Valley, without a truck-road across it, and hot as the hinges all summer. But Lemoigne knew his mine was rich and he was willing to wait; though every so often he offered to sell out cheap, so he could go back and die in Paris.

Many experts and promoters—and capitalists, too—toiled across Death Valley, through the wide portals of Cottonwood Canyon, and up to his humble camp. They inspected his mine, and some had made him good offers for it, but Old John turned them all down. Even a certified check was nothing to him—he wanted the cash in his hand. He was a dreamy sort of fellow, quite content to live alone and let the world go by.

To get to his camp from Darwin I engaged a Shoshone Indian for a guide; and figured that, for once, I wouldn't get lost. An Indian is supposed to know the country, and the Shoshones are reputed to know hundreds of hidden springs which a white man would walk right by. Charley Wrinkle was his name and a more good-natured fellow I never hope to see. Always laughing—but he did get lost.

We camped the night before at Emigrant Spring and in the morning Charley's horse was gone. His fine horse, that he had paid twenty dollars for—and he brought him in about noon. All the burros were packed, we were just ready to start, when I spotted Charley pouring the last of the water out of our two-gallon canteen.

"What's the matter, Charley?" I inquired, and he laughed.

"Too heavy," he answered.

"How long ago you go over this trail?"

"Oh, long time. Maybeso ten years."

"Yes. Maybeso that trail all washed out now. You better fill up that canteen."

All right, Charley was willing. He filled it up again and we went down Emigrant Wash until we could look right across and see Lemoigne's Canyon. It is the first one south of Cottonwood, and an old Indian trail went up to it. All that lay between was about five miles of sun-blackened boulders where the cloudbursts had washed them down. In a *few* million years they had brought down quite a lot of rock, and we had to cross all those washes.

But that was easy—for Charley. He knew the place on the other side where the trail came out; and Short Man—Shorty Harris—had shirt-tailed the route by tying white rags on the bushes. Everything was easy for Charley, but we got a late start and the sun was quite low before we started up the steep mountain. The burros began to grunt and groan, Charley got off his old horse and walked. Then the sun went down, it got dark and we hadn't reached the mine.

From the mine it was two or three miles further, down the trail to Lemoigne's camp, so we decided we'd better camp. In the darkness the burros might get off the trail and then we *would* be lost. There was lots of fine filaree grass where it had sprouted after the last rain, a couple of years before, and we had everything we needed with us. Our beds, lots of grub, canned tomatoes—everything.

We took a good drink from the two-gallon canteen, poured out about a quart for each of the animals and let them drink theirs from the wash-basin. Then we hobbled them out, to feed all night on the nice *alfileria*—and in the morning every one of them was there. After a good sup of water they were satisfied to eat instead of taking the back trail home.

"Pretty good—having water!" laughed Charley. But the next time he will do it again. Throw out all the water because it is too heavy. Too much—make burro's back sore.

We found Lemoigne's Mine on the face of the ridge looking out over Death Valley; but it was hard to believe that, after holding it forty years, he had got so little work done. It was strictly a one-man proposition. Instead of setting up a windlass and hiring a man to hoist he had made a series of benches on an incline and shovelled the ore up from bench to bench. Incredible labor, and very little to show for it.

But there was another reason why he was slow—the mine was bone-dry. After bringing in his winter's supply of provisions he packed water on his burros up the steepest zig-zag trail in America until the snow began to fall. Then he melted up enough to fill three or four barrels with water and went ahead on his assessment work. In December he worked on one group for the year that was about to expire, then he worked in January on another group to hold it for the following year.

There was very little time left for real development work, and sometimes it didn't snow at all. Not for a year or so. None of his holes were over twenty feet deep, but they showed he had the ore. It was only when the promoters began to figure on a road and trucking it out to the railroad, that their enthusiasm waned. When Rhyolite and Skidoo were in their glory he received some good offers for his mine, but he never made a sale. It would take a pack-train to carry the money in to him, and he wouldn't accept a check. The truth is, he was satisfied to live there all alone, with the feeling that he was worth a million dollars.

We drove our burros down his zig-zag trail, and it was evident that Lemoigne was no roadmaker. That trail was so steep and had so many short turns in it that the burros went on strike. Their packs kept slipping down over their ears—it was just a one-way trail. Everything was packed *up*—it was not intended to pack down. His burros always returned with empty saddles.

But when we reached the bottom we received a royal welcome, though the old man was far from happy. Some cowmen had invaded his solitude and located a herd of cattle on his water. His paradise had been trampled into the dust, he had been compelled to build fences around his tent-houses, and all the feed was gone. He had threatened to shoot the cowboys, but they were within their rights and had promised to do as much for him.

It was a delicate situation, and for the first two hours he could talk of nothing else but his troubles. Then his native calm returned, he inquired about the war and what was going on in the world—and then he got to his mine. It was worth a million yet, but he was seventy-seven years old and had held it for forty years. All he wanted for it now was twenty-five thousand—just enough to live out his life.

Why should he poison his remaining days by fighting with these cattlemen, who were trying to take the whole country? It would be better to sell out and go. All this quarrelling and fighting was not for a man like him—what he needed was peace and quiet. A rest. Life was more than making money and, after the war was over, he could go back to Paris, to die. There was only one thing that counted to an old man like him, and that was health. He no longer said "Good-bye" or "Good luck" to his friends. All he wished them when they departed was "Good health."

When we left the next day he wished us "Good health," but he did not return to Paris to die. That very next summer he saddled up his burros and went down into the Valley of Death, on his way to Rhyolite. Perhaps he felt his end approaching, perhaps he was out of his head. At Hole-In-The-Rock Spring he camped and his burros pulled out in the night, but Old John was wise to their ways and he found them at Furnace Creek Ranch.

Oscar Denton, the ranch boss, was there alone and he warned the old man to turn back.

"I have buried eleven men who have died from the heat," he said, "and I don't want to bury you."

"Have no fear for me," answered Lemoigne, politely. "I have lived in this country for over forty years. I understand how to cross."

He went on with his burros and, a few days later, a prospector found him, dead. Death Valley had claimed him at last.

Chapter Ten

Shorty Harris

Shorty Harris was a real "single blanket jackass prospector" as the bronze plate on his tombstone announces—a man who spent fifty years of his life rambling after his "asses," and who is credited with finding five rich mines. Yet there are those who say that he never found a mine—that it was always some other man who made the strike while Shorty took the credit.

But even they have to acknowledge this—he never refused a lift to a man who was broke. That is why he had them with him. And when he made a sale he bought the drinks for everybody until his last dollar was gone. He lived, not for money, but for renown and acclaim and the admiration of the multitude. When he sold the Bullfrog for nine hundred dollars it was his boast that he had more people following after him than a Salvation Army Captain.

He was a simple-minded fellow, when all is said and done; no match for the unscrupulous promoters who grabbed hold of him every time he made a strike. But he was a picturesque character, with an odd sense of humor—no talker, but a great man to coin phrases. His story of the discovery of Bullfrog is typical of the way he got rich, and broke, always passing it off with a laugh.

"I was staying at the Keane Wonder Mine in the summer of 1904 when it petered out. The boys who were working there all decided to go to Goldfield, which was booming. But one fellow named Ed Cross was left behind, broke. He was newly married—had a nice wife inside—and he said to me:

" 'Shorty, you see how I'm fixed, but I want to get to Goldfield. Take me along, and I'll pay you when I can.'

" 'All right,' I says, 'as long as there's flour in the sack you can have half of it.'

"He went along with me, and we camped where Bullfrog is now. I discovered the mine, and it was very rich ore—turquoise blue, with green and gold. It was too good to send to the mint. They sealed it in oil-cans and shipped it to jewelers all over the world. A rich lord, from England, had a setting of it in his ring.

"Well, I let Cross in on it, we staked it, and went on to Goldfield. There was a saloon-keeper there who took me in. He kept me in a private house, away from my friends, for three weeks, and I was drunk all the time. Until I signed away my claim, for one thousand dollars. It was sworn before a notary —six witnesses against my single signature. Ed Cross held on to his claim until the camp got to booming and sold out just in time, for big money. Now he owns a hundred and twenty acres of fine orange-and-walnut land near Santa Ana.

"I lived on beans and champagne in Tonopah for four weeks, and staked everybody that touched me for a loan. I treated everybody that came along to the drinks and the eats. There was a chili joint there that biled the beans for me in oil-cans, and all down the table we had bottles of champagne. I was drunk all the time and never knew what happened, until the last of my money was gone. All I got for my mine was one thousand dollars and three barrels of whiskey. I drank the whiskey."

This is the way the story goes when told by Frank P. Mannix, Editor of *The Bullfrog Miner,* in an article in *Harper's Weekly,* April 11, 1908.

"The Bullfrog, like most mining camps, has its romantic story of discovery. Early in the month of August, 1904, Shorty Harris, whose Christian name has been lost in the nicknaming custom which obtains among miners, packed his burros and started out from Goldfield with Ballarat, California, his objective point of destination. He was travelling along the Amargosa Desert when he came upon Edward Cross, a stranded prospector, and the two camped at Buck Springs.

"An outcropping of rock attracted Harris's attention and while waiting for Cross to recuperate for the journey he climbed up a declivity and broke off a piece of the formation. It showed free gold, and so soon as Cross was able to travel the prospectors secured other specimens and returned to Goldfield. Assays showed seven hundred dollars in gold to the ton and a stampede immediately followed. The entire country proved to be highly mineralized and some of the best mines in the State have been developed there.

"The naming of the district came from one of those characteristic small incidents common to mining life. A bullfrog never croaked within hundreds of miles of its boundaries but the predominating color of the richest ore found in the district is alternate dark and green, which is well-defined in every specimen. A lump of the formation comparative in size and shape with the animal very much resembles a bullfrog. While Harris and Cross were debating a name for the new camp a lump of ore was tipped over and it rolled down to the side of Harris. It so much resembled a bullfrog that the new district was then and there given the name."

This sounds a little different from Shorty's own account, but compare it with the statement of a real old-timer who has lived around Death Valley for years:

"Shorty Harris never located a mine in his life. He was heading for Goldfield when he passed the Keane Wonder Mine; and Ed Cross, who was quitting, asked him if he could put his bed-roll on a burro. Shorty said: Yes, he could go with him clear to Goldfield.

"They camped at Mud Spring, near Bullfrog, and Shorty had a cache of grub stored with Judge Beatty, so he told Ed to stay there while he went and got it—it would take him six or seven hours. Ed was wandering around on that big ledge when he knocked off a piece of rock that showed gold. They located it together and went on to Goldfield where Pat O'Brien, the saloon-keeper, got Shorty drunk and bought his share for nine hundred dollars.

"Shorty took the nine hundred and bought beer by the barrel for the boys until it was all gone. Ed Cross held on to his share and finally sold it for twenty or thirty thousand dollars. Ed was a quiet guy, and if you would ask him didn't Shorty find the mine he would probably say: 'Yes. Shorty found it.'

"But he told me the real story, and I know."

The only way to know anything about these mining discoveries is to go to just one man. If you go to two, what you know is reduced by half. Go to three and you don't know anything. Shorty swore off after he went broke at Tonopah and went back to his old stamping-ground—not Death Valley, but Ballarat and the Panamint Mountains. His description of the discovery of Harrisburg is brief and to the point.

"After losing the price of my half interest in Bullfrog I went across Death Valley and found Harrisburg. I picked up Pete Aguereberry on the way. He was travelling with two other fellows and I had a pardner at Rhyolite—Sam Driscoll. That made five people having an interest in the hill.

"Aguereberry and I finally divided it up, north and south, but it was a one-man proposition and Pete never would sign anything. We were offered one hundred and fifteen thousand dollars by an English Company with headquarters at Denver. The money was in the bank waiting, whenever Aguereberry signed. But he wouldn't sign—he wanted a million! Later on he refused to extend an option and our mining-man quit and left us flat. Then I formed a company with my half of the hill, and my millionaire promoter cleaned me.

"Harrisburg was a gold proposition and we had sixty thousand in sight. I took forty-two thousand shares for a home-stake, not noticing that the stock was assessable, and they froze me out. Voted an assessment of two cents a share. I quit stock companies, right there."

Shorty told this story in a detached sort of way, as if it was something that might happen to anybody; but Pete Aguere-berry is French and excitable and when he talked he put his heart into it.

"I was the original discoverer of Harrisburg and the North Star Mine, but Shorty Harris took all the credit. I threw in with him at Furnace Creek Ranch. Never saw him before, but we were both going to Ballarat by the Wet Trail over the mountain, so we travelled together.

"When we came to the black hill where Harrisburg now is Shorty pointed to the big vein of copper-stained rock that runs through the hill and said it was barren. He said the country was no good—the formation was wrong—nothing but lime, schist and slicks. I got off and looked at the rock, but Shorty was in a hurry to get to Wild Rose and he went on.

"The first piece of rock I broke off showed pin-points of gold, and the next was full of it. I looked that hill over for an hour or two, but I didn't stake it. Shorty wasn't my pardner but he was with me, and when I saw him walking behind his burros I felt sorry for him. I didn't need to give him anything, but he had been beat out of his Bullfrog Mine and I decided to let him in on it.

"He had gone ahead and was mad as hell because I had kept him waiting. When he saw me coming he started his burros on again and when I hollered he wouldn't stop. He wanted to get to the water, eleven miles away. When I finally caught up with him he wouldn't talk. I said:

" 'What do you think of this rock, Shorty?'

"But he wouldn't look. Finally glanced at it and threw it away.

" 'No good,' he says.

" 'It's full of gold!' I said.

" 'You're crazy,' he comes back.

[*91*]

"Finally he took a look through his magnifying glass and jumped up into the air.

" 'Where'd you get that rock?' he yelled.

" 'Back in that black hill,' I said.

" 'Aw, that country is no good—nothing but sand, schist and slicks.'

" 'All the same,' I said, 'I found it there. And the whole vein is full of gold.'

"Shorty kept looking at the rock through his glass and getting more and more excited.

" 'They beat me out of Bullfrog,' he would say, 'but now I'm going to show 'em.'

"I made him promise not to say anything until we went back and staked the ground—I agreed to give him the south side of the hill and take the north, myself. When we came to Wild Rose there were six old-timers camped at the water—Frank Kennedy, Old Man Thurman, Judge Curran, Jack Byrne and two more—and Shorty was very much excited. He kept saying he had struck something that would make Bullfrog look like nothing. I was afraid to leave him away from me, because we hadn't staked the ground yet.

"We were going back the next morning at daylight, but the burros pulled out on us in the night. I was so excited I couldn't sleep—lay awake all night and got up three hours before dawn. I intended to get the animals and beat it, before Shorty told, but my saddle burro was gone. At last I drove his burros in for him and told him to go back and stake claims for both of us while I went to Ballarat and got some grub.

"We were both broke and out of grub, but I was expecting a check, due in Ballarat the first of the month. When I got to Ballarat the check hadn't come. I had no money—never had begged so I just camped and waited. After three days the storekeeper noticed me and said to his clerk:

" 'Go out and see what's the matter with that fellow. He hasn't had a fire in three days. If he's just out of grub, tell him he can have all he wants on credit.'

"The clerk came out, and it was true. I had nothing to cook, so I had not lit a fire for three days, waiting for the check. Well, when the man told me that, I was glad and went up to the store. But I did not like to ask for grub on credit before all those men. The store was crowded, so I waited around all day, expecting that they would go—but it was dark and the store-keeper was getting ready to close up before he noticed me.

"He gave me a drink and a lot of grub on credit, but while I had been waiting in the store I had heard the men talking about a big strike that had been made by a Frenchman—French Pete. They didn't know who I was, and this was the first news I had that our discovery was known, but that night I heard Thurman say:

" 'I'm going up to that new strike.'

"Another fellow said that he was, too. They all decided to go. They went out into the night, caught up their horses and burros, packed them with grub and beat it. I was waiting for the check to pay for my grub; but when I heard them start out, I went too. When I got to Harrisburg the whole hill was staked and men were everywhere.

"I looked on the north side of the hill and my stakes were gone. Somebody had pulled them up and relocated the ground. Then Thurman came and asked who I was, and I told him I was French Pete and I had discovered that mine, and before I would let anybody take it away from me I would fight and either leave my bones or another man's on the ground.

"Shorty Harris had gone to Emigrant Spring for water and these men didn't know me, but finally Frank Kennedy said if I had found the mine I was entitled to half of it. So they pull-ed up the stakes and let me put back mine. A lot of men rushed into the country and Shorty sold out to a millionaire from Los Angeles. He organized a big company, paid Shorty in stock, then voted ten cents a share assessment and froze him out.

[*93*]

Shorty had thirty-five thousand shares, and no money to pay.

"I had my mine sold once for one hundred and eighty thousand but litigation tied up the title for two years and I have never been able to sell. Now the pipe-line that Bob Montgomery built from Telescope Peak to Skidoo is being taken up and my water supply is cut off. I have to pack it seven miles, from Emigrant Spring. I have ten thousand dollars' worth of ore on the dump, thousands of tons blocked out, three groups of silver and lead claims near by, and am willing to sell out reasonable. Everybody says I am too high-priced, but now I am willing to sell.

"This is not the first mine I have owned. I was the fourth man on the ground in the Tonopah rush, and got a lease with two other men. A few feet down, it opened out two feet wide, and along the hanging-wall in the burnt-out iron there were balls of silver as big as buckshot.

"So many people came to look that we could hardly work, and they packed off half the ore for samples. A big German came and looked it over and offered me ten thousand for my third interest. This was easy money, as I had only been on the ground eight days, but other leasers had got as much as fifty thousand for theirs, and I had the ore in sight.

"I refused, and asked twenty thousand. The German offered thirteen thousand and I told him I would meet him downtown, the next day. But I delayed, and when I got to the saloon, he was gone. Well, I didn't care and I was going off when I met him in the street. The German said he had to leave town for a week, but he would give me fifteen thousand cash for my share.

"Something told me to take it, but my pardners had kicked on having a German in with them and so I turned him down. The German said all right, that was his top price, and beat it. Two days later our vein began to pinch out. It pinched down to a talc-streak, but the walls still held true and slippery—only no values. We sank on it sixty feet and it opened out wide again, but barren. We decided to drift on the vein, then we cross-cut east and west, but no values. All the time I was hollering to sink—sink—but my pardners wouldn't do it. I said if they didn't I'd quit. All right, I quit. Two days later my pardners quit, too. Another man took the lease, sank three feet and struck silver in solid chunks. He made hundreds of thousands of dollars.

"Well, that is the way in this business. If it wasn't for my pardners I'd be rich."

So much for Bullfrog and Harrisburg, but Shorty had other mines—the St. Patrick and the World Beater, east of Ballarat; and another one, over near Gold Belt. That was very rich, too, what there was of it; but he had to leave pillars to support the hanging-wall, and while he was away somebody stole them for the ore and the whole roof caved in. The St. Patrick petered out; and as for the World Beater, that was found by an Indian, Panamint Tom. Or so they say.

"Tom was cutting wood when he discovered the outcropping and, since at that time an Indian could not locate a claim, he piled a cord of wood on top of it. When a white man came to get the wood Tom showed the gold to 'Short Man.' That is how Harris came to find it. He took in a man named Smalley and they worked it together for a while. The ore was so rich that, according to Shorty, you could pound out twenty dollar gold-pieces. It was worth more as specimens than it was for gold. Sold for eighteen dollars an ounce, quartz and all, but there was very little of it. The vein was only half an inch wide and you could bring down the results of a year's work in a cigar-box. Shorty sold out to Bob Montgomery, but don't ask me how much Tom got."

It really looks, if these old-timers are right, as if Shorty was under a kind of spell—some sort of a fairy charm or devil's curse which decreed that he should find much gold, but always through somebody else. He had travelled so far over the blinding desert sands that his eyes were bad. He could hardly recognize gold when he saw it, and he was always in such a hurry he would never stop to look. So the chances are that, but for the kindness of his heart in taking along strangers, he would never have found any mines at all.

But, though Shorty Harris was friendly enough, he was close-mouthed about his mines. He would talk about his burros and what a curse they were on his life—always slipping away and all that—but around Ballarat he would tell you nothing. So in 1918, catching him broke and in need of a stake, I hired him and his pack-train to take me up to see Scotty, and get some good pictures on the way.

It was in the dead of winter, and bitter cold on the high ground, and for three days he said practically nothing; but down at Surveyors' Well, where we laid over for a day, I received help from a fellow author. In the old shack by the well a clutter of rough-paper magazines had been left by a former occupant and Shorty was looking them over with his heat-blurred eyes when he suddenly hurled one to the floor.

"What the hell is the matter with this feller?" he howled. "Here's a story about old Panamint, and he has it out on the plain! On a plain, mind ye, when everybody knows its clear up on the top of a mountain!"

"Oh, never mind that," I said. "He's a good writer—I know him—and he just wanted to use the name. So he took a town down on the desert and changed the name to Panamint."

"But he has the damned town in the bottom of Death Valley —on the other side of the mountains!"

"Poetic license! All our best writers do it. Geography means nothing to them."

"But he's got a parson here—the parson of Panamint—and there never was a preacher in the camp!"

Shorty was all het up, shaken out of his three days' silence, and he went on to tell me what an old-timer he was. He had been leaded at Leadville, crippled at Cripple Creek, raw-hided out of Rawhide, and so on down the line. He had even pound-

SHORTY HARRIS

real "single blanket jackass prospector." Credited with the discovery of five rich mines.

(Photograph by Dane Coolidge)

STOVE PIPE HOLE IN 1918.

It was named by Frank Kennedy after some stovepipe which the emigrants left there.

THE DESERT QUEEN AT BALLARAT.

When the old-time prospectors were hunting for their burros they found gold, and when they were hunting for gold they found their burros. Since they have taken to Fords they don't find anything. *(Photograph by Dane Coolidge)*

Scotty's Castle

in Grapevine Canyon, at the upper end of Death Valley. It cost over two million dollars.

(*Photograph by Dane Coolidge*)

ed a drill in the Coffin Mine, in the Funeral Range, on the graveyard shift, and had quit when they put him to work with a blanket-stiff. This started him off—he became friendly, confidential; and, before he got through, without meaning to at all, he had told the story of his life.

Shorty Harris was born in Providence, Rhode Island, and worked for almost nothing in the cotton-mills until he was big enough to start west. He was heading for the boom mining camp of Leadville when he went broke and had to take a job, digging potatoes. He earned good money, for workers were scarce, and it was here his first romance blossomed—and died.

The daughter of the boss was working in the fields—a fair-haired, laughing girl who used to play jokes on him and bean him with a potato when he got too gay. It was love at first sight and as soon as he got rich, he promised to come back and marry her. But he didn't get rich—and when he fell into the rush and excitement of the mining town he never even wrote. First he was waiting for some good news to tell her. Then he put it off because it had been so long, and because he was not getting ahead. Then he moved on and forgot her address. But he never forgot the girl—no, never.

Shorty followed the mining booms west until he came to the great State of Nevada, but it was in the desert mountains west of Death Valley that he finally settled down to be a prospector. He was a little man, scarcely five feet tall; and once, after making a sale, he had gone into Los Angeles and had his front teeth plated with gold. It was a fine job of blacksmithing and cost him five hundred dollars, and certainly gave him a golden smile.

He kept his burros shod, to distinguish their tracks from those of the wild burros; but he drove them so hard they were always sneaking away from him, even when he fed them his bacon-rinds. He was widely known for his burro jokes, and firmly believed they could understand every word that was said. When he was camping at Stone Corral, Old Man Gillian, the prospector, came through asking how long he would be there.

"Psst, not so loud!" said Shorty. "The damned burros might hear you. I'm going out in the marning."

But the burros always knew, and in the morning they would be gone. Then he would set out at dawn to trail them, and come back blazing mad. No matter how much he hobbled them and side-lined them, they would pull out after dark and travel all night, hopping back worn and weary to begin the long day's hike. But when he got them under the packs he drove them mercilessly, until they reached the next water.

The biggest and meanest burro of all was Pinto, but one day he got bit on the nose by a rattlesnake and for once he came back to camp. His teeth were clenched tight, his eyes closed, his head swelled, but he returned to his master for help. Shorty rubbed permanganate of potassium into the wound and bathed his sore head with coal-oil. Then he put some more oil on a swab and pushed it down his throat. Old Pinto never kicked—just stood and held his head out until the job was done. Then he went away and was gone for three weeks. When he came back he was all right, with a big scar on his nose, and just as mean as ever.

One of Shorty's favorite sayings was that he was too light for heavy work and too heavy for light work, but he seldom rode a burro. He walked, driving the pack-train before him. When he picked up a rock the rear animals almost flew, and so he kept them on the run. If he had stopped they would have laid down under the packs. And when they got over halfway on their day's journey they would hurry ahead of their own accord, in order to get rid of their loads.

When Shorty was happy he would sing his favorite tune:

> *"I never will forget*
> *The days when we were young*
> *Ta-ra—ta-ra.*
> *It don't seem so very long ago*
> *Ta-ra-rum—ta-ra-rum."*

But he was living in a rough country, and most of his jokes were grim. Especially when he told about the heat.

"I've seen it so hot in Death Valley," he said, "the water in my canteen was biling. Do you know what all the ducks and geese do when they fly over Death Valley? They pack canteens. Or that's what a saloon-keeper told a man over in Rhyolite when he saw him stringing beer bottles on a rope. What he needed was two two-gallon canteens. I mind one time I was going down Emigrant Wash in the summer time when I saw a big man ahead—and he was rambling, too. Going from bush to bush and trying to dig a hole for shade, but the bushes were all too small for him.

" 'Now what will I do?' I said; and I got out my prospector's pick from the box, just before he ran up and tried to grab me.

" 'Water! Water!' he says; but I warned him off and threatened to brain him with the pick. He was far gone—his mouth was open and his tongue stuck out a little, like a horn-toad's.

" 'Sure I'll give you water,' I said, 'but don't you try to grab me or I'll kill you.'

" 'All right,' he says. 'But for God's sake, hurry up.'

"So I gave him a drink from my canteen, but I held on to it by the straps and when I thought he had had enough I jerked it away from him. In about two minutes I gave him another drink. Then I loaded him onto my riding burro and headed back for Emigrant Spring. It was twelve miles up there, and hot, but I gave him a few swallows at a time and got him in alive.

"He was a man named Rankin, but I forgot all about him, until one day I was up in Goldfield when I met him on the street. His face seemed familiar, but I couldn't place him. He stopped and looked at me and said:

" 'Ain't you Shorty Harris?'

"He was the same big man I'd met in Emigrant Wash, and he was master-mechanic on the Belmont Mine—one of the best. Well, sir, he tried to give me everything he had, he was so grateful for what I had done."

[*99*]

Shorty is one of the old-timers who insists that the heat creates gas.

"In hot weather," he said, "a kind of gas rises from the holes in the salt-bed at the bottom of Death Valley. It looks like a white mist on a frosty morning—hangs low along the ground. I was crossing one time when I saw it myself, and I was about all in. I had something like the blind-staggers, but I came out all right. The effect of great heat is to make a man's legs give way—make him want to lie down and get in the shade. And the sun will take your hide off, I don't care how tanned you are.

"I crossed the Valley in the summer one time and the next day my face peeled like a snake. The skin came off in chunks. Mike Lane crossed Death Valley in July, and when he got to Rhyolite he was burnt red. There was a newspaper feller there and he thought he would get a story out of Mike.

" 'Was it very hot in Death Valley?' he said.

" 'Yes,' says Mike. 'In the mesquite trees down by Stove-pipe Hole I saw two chuckawalla lizards, and they were spitting on their toes to get them cool.'

"That shut the reporter up."

Well, Shorty was good at telling stories—and he certainly was an old-time desert-man—but on that trip to Scotty's Ranch he got hopelessly lost. He didn't know whether Mesquite Spring was down in the wash or up on the side of Grapevine Mountain, and he had hired out for a guide.

We knew it was going to be a hard day's ride so, after laying over a day to rest up the burros, we left Surveyors' Well at dawn. Our road was supposed to go straight up Lost Valley to Mesquite Spring, a distance of twenty miles; but as nobody travelled it and the cloudbursts had washed out the tracks, the question was—which way was it from Surveyors' Well?

Surveyors' Well lies on the floor of the Valley, just a hole in the ground surrounded by big mesquite trees, half-buried in drifting sands. Shorty said that the road was towards the east, along the edge of the Grapevine Mountains which loomed up like a solid wall. So we went east until we cut what was left of a wagon-road and followed it to the north.

It was heading towards the gap in the mountains ahead where the drainage from the north country comes in, but it was rough. Over a thousand low ridges and washes—and the further we went the rougher it got. It split up into wagon-tracks, some of which turned back while the rest rambled crazily on—but anyhow, we were traveling north.

According to the map of the United States Geological Survey, Mesquite Spring lay in the pass where Tin Mountain and the Grapevine Range come together. The burros began to grunt and smell of the ground, looking for a soft place to lie down; but there were no soft places, it was nothing but rocks, and Shorty drove them on inexorably. Our road had petered out to a dim trail, the sun was well over to the west, when, high up on the slope of Grapevine Mountain, I saw what appeared to be a grove of tall trees, rising up out of a narrow canyon.

I found out later it was the shadows cast by the overhang of the undermined north wall. But when I asked Shorty if there was a spring up there he said he didn't know. When pressed further he finally admitted that he didn't know where Mesquite Spring was. It had been eighteen years since he had come through the country, and everything was changed. I showed him the map and he declared profanely he wouldn't use it to start a fire.

We finally decided to keep on going north, but the burros were getting thirsty and beginning to suck their tongues, turning fretfully from side to side. They knew we were lost and they wanted to turn back, but we kept on until it got dark. Then we came to a broad wash, smooth and level and good going. If we had turned west instead of east from Surveyors' Well we would have been in it all the way.

There were burro-tracks in this wash and, down the middle of it, a wagon had recently passed. Everything looked good for finding the spring pretty soon, but even Shorty was getting tired. I finally told him I would walk as long as he would, but any time he wanted to make a dry camp it was all right with me. It was about eight o'clock, the burros had found their strength again and we plodded soberly on, when Shorty called a halt.

We camped by some mesquite trees behind a low hill and, after throwing off the packs, Shorty hobbled the burros and sidelined them. Then, seeing them start off up the wash together, he brought them all back and tied them fast to the trees with their pack-ropes.

"They always do it," he complained. "I never knew it to fail, when I got good and lost, my burros always pulled out on me."

Well, Shorty was good and lost. He didn't know yet whether Mesquite Spring was ahead somewhere or up on the side of Grapevine Mountain. He was afraid we would pass by it in the night and so he camped, right there. Though he had a two-gallon canteen full of water and had been sweating all day, he refused to take a drink and went to bed dry. I had a quart and drank half of it, for I felt sure the spring was close.

All that night I could hear the burros trying to break down the mesquite trees and fighting against their ropes, and I got up at the first peep of dawn. Climbing the low hill I looked up the wash and there, not a quarter of a mile ahead, was a huge bunch of mesquite trees. The ground all around them was white with alkali, sure sign it was a spring.

"Here's your Mesquite Spring!" I shouted down to Shorty; and he came up on the run. We had been camping all night within a few hundred yards of water. The burros had smelled it and fought their ropes—but their bonds had held them fast. When Shorty saw the spring he raised both hands to the sky and cursed. Then he ran back to camp, grabbed up his canteen and poured every drop into the sand.

"You'd better wait," I said, "until we get up to that spring. It may have a dead horse in it."

But no! Dry as he was, Shorty did not even take a drink; just threw on the packs and beat it. Right there I lost the last of my respect for the intelligence of desert-guides. He was the third one I had hired, the third one to get lost, and the third one to pour out all his water.

We camped at the spring and had breakfast and, just as we started up the wash, we met Walter Scott, himself. He had come down from his ranch to re-locate some platinum claims, and told us to go right on up. For five days we stayed at his tent-house, the weather being bad and Scotty full of entertaining tales; and, though Shorty's burros were in good feed and his pay was going right on, he was in a terrible hurry to start off again. He wanted to go somewhere, to be on his way, and as we packed to leave—on a seven-mile trip that we could make in two hours—Scotty pulled a good one.

"Shorty," he said, "you burro-men are all the same. You take the slowest means of transportation there is and then you're always in a hurry. You remind me of a story I heard in Italy when I was travelling with the Wild West Show.

"The snail's wife was sick and he went for the doctor. It took him twenty years to get there and twenty more to get back. He had just crossed the road when a wagon went by and the wheel nearly crushed him.

" 'There!' " he said. " 'If I hadn't been in such a hurry, that wagon would have run right over me!' "

Scotty laughed to high heaven at this joke, and Shorty was mad all day.

We hurried down the wash to Mesquite Spring and had to camp until the next day. Then we were off at dawn, following down the wide wash on a good wagon track that passed within a mile of Surveyors' Well. The third day we got clear to Furnace Creek Ranch, and the next day we camped at Eagle Borax. When we toiled up over the mountain and reached old Panamint he was in a greater rush than ever, but the burros pulled out on him that night and were half-way to Ballarat before he caught them and flogged them back.

That was Shorty—always in a hurry. But he kept ahead of the slow wagon-wheel of Death, and never got run over or killed. He died of old age, and the infirmities of age; but before he passed away he dictated this epitaph:

> *"Bury me beside Jim Dayton in the Valley we loved.*
> *Above me write: 'Here lies Shorty Harris,*
> *a single blanket jackass prospector.' "*

You can see it beside the road to the Eagle Borax Works, where Dayton perished in the heat.

In life, Shorty had failed of his great ambition to be known as Death Valley's greatest prospector, but in death he achieved that renown. When he went to his grave he had more people following after him than a Salvation Army Captain.

Chapter Eleven

Death Valley Scotty

The biggest man in Death Valley is Scotty. Whether he has a mine or not, whether he ever had a mine or not, he overshadows the rest of the prospectors the way his castle does a tent-house. No matter if the castle isn't his, or if he gets all his money from Johnson, he is just naturally *big* and he has picked the right place to be big in. He was King there when it was an empty desert, and he is still King when it is overrun with automobiles and tourists.

The first question people ask when you come back from Death Valley is:

"Did you see Scotty?"

If you did, your vacation was a success. If not you are just another tourist. And if he showed you over his castle, as he does sometimes, and told you a lot of funny stories, your social popularity is assured. People will swarm to shake the hand that shook the hand of Scotty, and all the poisonous hate which the old-timers give off will go by you like cigarette smoke. It is easy to get cynical and say he is a faker—he is still the one and only Scotty!

Under the circumstances a man would have a nerve to sit in Judgment on Our Hero, a cowboy who has ridden broncs before the crowned heads of Europe, to whom the King of Spain gave a cigar. Buffalo Bill was glad to have him as one of his Big Six cowboys; and when, after eleven years, he fired him, for Scotty life had just begun. He went back to Death

Valley, which he had entered as a boy, and never gave up till he found his Lost Mine or a financial equivalent of the same.

Wherever the money came from, his clothes were full of big bills; and every time he told the world he was broke—he laughed. He was the darling of the gods, the familiar friend of millionaires and a winner with the ladies. No matter what the future may hold for him he is sitting pretty, up to date. There is nothing small about Scotty but his feet. He is accustomed to do everything in a big way; and he admits that, while he can't spell, he can think!

As for his spelling, he has gone through life with certain preconceived ideas, such as that tHe spells "the"; but William Shakspeare spelled his own name three different ways and never let it cramp his style. On the day before Walter's father was going to send him to school he ran away and started west. He hated all school-marms and people who tried to tell him things, and has hated them ever since. Never try to tell Scotty anything. *Listen,* and let him tell *you* something.

Walter Scott was born in Kentucky about 1870 and, far from being an ignorant hill-billy, he is descended from a long line of blue-bloods. His father was the owner of a string of race horses and young Walter spent his boyhood in the company of jockeys and swipes, from whom he learned much worldly wisdom. But when he was eight years old he ran away from home and landed at Wells, Nevada.

There he became a cowboy and a good one and at an early age he got a job with Buffalo Bill's Wild West Show, riding broncs and doing the Pony Express. Of those exciting days he says:

"Buffalo Bill hated cowboys and loved Indians, Cossacks and all the rest of the riders that went to make up his show. The result was we got the worst of it every time there was a fight, and we were working on each other all the time. The performers had a kind of Kangaroo Court where offenders were tried, but they could not levy a fine or sentence the hands to punishment—just recommend the punishment to Bill.

"Riders were paid fifty dollars a week, of which ten was held out until they quit or got fired, or the end of the season came. So they always had a stake when it was time to go, and everything was found when we were working. There were generally about twenty-five bronc riders, and half of them were always hurt or lame. They rode every day instead of once in several days the way these Rodeo hands do.

"The thing that made the Bill Show so good was that everything was genuine—real Indians, Cossacks, Gauchos and English Drill Corps. Oro Peso was the finest roper the world has ever seen. He was a big, handsome, high-class Mexican, and the only man who could make a loop spread out and get bigger as he threw it. He used a *maguey* rope—not a cotton sash-cord, the way these rope-spinners do today—and they all learned their stuff from watching him.

"He was a sure shot with the rope and the riders always felt safe when they saw him standing by the pens. If a man would get hung up and drug, Oro Peso's loop would catch the horse by the fore feet and stop him. Once a woman rider got thrown and hung up in her stirrup. The horse was running and kicking back at her. Oro forefooted the horse just as it came to a gate. It knocked the gate open, turned a houlihan and fell through into a lot where a hundred crack soldiers were drilling. They all leapt on that horse at once and held it down while the girl was released and carried away. She must have been badly hurt, because she never came back.

"I used to put on a fancy stunt with a horse that would jump ten feet high. He just bounced up and down and shook them all off. I went up with him, jerked my feet out of the stirrups and landed away off to one side, bowing. A horse will kick you when you land behind him, or even off to one side, but I could tell what he was going to do. A bronc has his hind legs far apart when he is bucking, close together when he is fixing to kick you. I got kicked in the solar plexus once. It sounded like a big, bass drum and put me in the hospital. Lots of times they would kick your leg from behind. They broke mine once.

"George Burch was the Chief of Cowboys and called out the men to ride next. There were seven chutes or pens in front of the grandstand and an Englishman with a plug hat and split-tail coat had charge of the mounts, which were given out by lots. Each man then took his bronc to its pen and with a helper saddled it to go. But these broncs were educated and knew lots of dirty tricks. They hated the riders, as they were rode by them every day, and did their best to kill us.

"The man who was called first got a break, but the last riders were out of luck. Their mounts would fight and rear, getting more nervous all the time, and when they were turned loose they went to pieces. Some could hardly be mounted at all. I would fool them by having my helper take his left foot out of the stirrup while holding the horse's head. Then I would put my foot in the empty stirrup, jump clear over his horse's rump and land astride the bronc.

"If I could catch him going up that was fine, but if he was coming down I lost out and fell. All I needed to ride was one stirrup—the right one—and I got to be an expert on stepping off when a horse threw himself or turned a houlihan."

This lasted for eleven years, but in the winter when the Show was closed, Scotty went back to Death Valley to look for a lost mine—Scotty's Mine. The float from this ledge had been discovered by old prospectors, who had gone in with the original Death Valley Expedition which first surveyed the Valley. This piece of quartz broke up the whole expedition for several days, while all hands prospected the neighboring hills for gold; but Scotty sketched the landmarks and later came back every winter, trying to trace that ore to its source.

Then one spring he reported for duty at the Show a little late and was fired. Broke and far from home, he remembered the horse-loving millionaire friends whose acquaintance he had made at the Show. That is, he remembered *them*—he never could remember their names. So, like a lost dog, he hurried to a great office building and stood by the elevator until the starter recognized him and told him his tall friend had moved.

This friend was Julius Gerard, and when Scotty found him he touched him for fifty dollars. At that time the mining excitement in Nevada was at its height and, when Scotty told him about his lost mine, Gerard offered to grubstake him if he would sign the usual contract, which would give him half of everything found.

Scotty returned to Death Valley and assembled the finest pack outfit that money could buy. He bought mules, and big mules, Government saddles and pack-outfits, and dropped out of sight for three years. At the end of that time he went back to New York and reported that he couldn't find the mine. He had spent eight thousand dollars and promised to pay it back, but Gerard was very nice about it and told him that that was not necessary. They had taken a chance together and had failed to find the mine. No repayment was called for, under their contract.

But Scott was not satisfied with that. He went on to Chicago, made the acquaintance of Albert M. Johnson, his present partner, and got a grubstake that was a grubstake. Johnson gave him twenty thousand for a starter and Scotty went right back to Mr. Gerard and tried to repay the eight thousand. But of course, being Scotty, he had to flash the whole roll and Gerard declined to be repaid. He suspected that Scott had found a mine and was trying to cover it up. They had words and the banker informed him he wanted one half of everything he had found. Scotty told him to go ahead and find it and he could have it *all*.

This started one of the grandest grubstake battles in the West, in which gold was flung into the streets time and again by Scotty and somebody hired a succession of scouts and Indians who tried to trail him to his mine. If the scouts were hired by Gerard that is not a matter of record—they might have been working on their own account. If they ever did find the mine, being of the wolf-breed they were, they would certainly never turn it over to some millionaire in return for their daily wage. In a very short time it became a case of dog eat dog, with no great scruples shown on either side, and in the next ten years Scotty led them a great chase, stopping every so often to go into town and throw some more gold in the streets.

Outsiders, not called in on the feud at all, made it their business to follow Mr. Scott. Then the shooting began, Scotty was ambushed three times and finally hired a bad Shoshone named Bob Black to help him hold up his end of the game. While drunk Bob had killed his wife and seven Paiutes at Ash Meadows and was on the dodge for his life. They made their headquarters in Scotty's Canyon, at the southern end of Black Mountain, and worked together for several years.

Then Black was killed and Scotty took on Bill Keyes, whom he accuses of leading his enemies to his hide-out and trying to get him killed. He had to move north after that, to the upper end of Death Valley, and he made Lost Wagons a deadline for Keyes which was respected for many years. In fact, Bill left the country and moved up to Colorado, but Scotty's troubles continued. He had so many enemies he never did know who was shooting at him.

In a sober moment, long afterwards, Scott confessed he never could figure out who they were or why they were trying to kill him. There were three different outfits whom he suspected—Bob Black, while he was alive; Alvord and Stiles, the train-robbers, whom he had taken in; and Antonio Apache, the leader of the Apache Scouts who made the last attempts to trail him. But he checked up on all of them afterwards and they came clear. It was somebody else, some man of mystery, who was not out to find his mine at all but to get revenge—to wipe him off the map. If he were after Scott's mine he would certainly not try to kill the only man who knew where it was. He was out for revenge, and Scotty thinks he is still trying to get him. Somebody in the background is always trying to stir up trouble, but nobody knows who it is.

At the end of about ten years of desert warfare, Scotty had been shot three times from ambush—once in the arm, once in the leg and once through the lungs, which laid him up for two months. In addition he had been snakebit twice and had his ear nipped by a hydrophobia skunk. Then the excitement died down, he quit riding into town with rolls of big bills and squandering them in riotous living. There were eleven years, he says, when he never saw a street-car—they had torn up the tracks in Goldfield.

But in those eleven years his companion on many a rough trip was Albert M. Johnson, the millionaire. They make a strange pair, for Johnson is almost fanatical in his religious views while Scotty is a hardened sinner. He is tough, and proud of it; while Johnson, according to his wife, never uttered an oath in his life. But, to keep up with Scott over the mountains and desert, he had to be all man.

Nobody can ride those ridges, even with a packer to handle the mules, without being in constant danger of his life. Anybody that will do it just for fun is certainly a dead-game sport. But Johnson rode the trails for twenty years, and took it as a joke. To Scotty he was always "my book-keeper," the man who held the sack while he went out after the "metal." To Johnson, Scotty was always "my care-taker," and so they passed it back and forth until nobody actually knew what their relationship was.

Nor do they know today. The old desert-men say it is easy—Scotty has got something on him. He can ask for ten thousand dollars any day, and get it. Well, that was true for the whole twenty years, until hard times laid a heavy hand on us all. But, though Johnson as far as is known dug up every dollar of the two million it took to build the castle, it is always "Scotty's Castle." With such exquisite courtesy does Johnson handle his "care-taker," that the world may never know.

Half the people in the United States thought that Scotty was dead and the other half thought he was broke. He had had enough of riotous living and savage chases across the desert. Settling down at Grapevine Canyon he led the life of an old-time frontiersman, riding the ridges with his mules while he killed mountain sheep, perhaps gathered up and hid more of his gold. For Scotty was foxy—he moved his gold twice. Once from the mine, wherever it was, and then from the cache where he had buried it.

In order to confuse his enemies he hid oil-cans full of water, and grain for his mules, in the most inaccessible places. Then, if he found he was being followed, he would throw a wide circle of a hundred miles or so and end up at one of these "tin-can springs." When his pursuers found the "spring" there was nothing left but empty cans, and it was always a long way from water. It is not unreasonable to suppose that some of these maddened trailers became the mysterious enemies who were out for nothing but revenge.

Having been chased for years and shot three times Scotty became ruthless in shaking off his enemies, and if some of them died before they reached water it would only give him a laughing sensation. He is a man quick to anger, with no mercy on a foe, and his bad habit of laughing them to scorn has made his enemies legion. All the old prospectors and desert men are against him and envious of his success, and every time he tells the papers he is broke they join in the Anvil Chorus.

Then he flashes another roll and does it all over again, until they turn bitter and go into the silence. But Scotty would not be happy without someone to hate, someone to hold up to public scorn and denounce as a pinchpenny piker. All the old-time storekeepers who over-charged him for a shirt have felt the rough edge of his tongue; and, if he could, he would "stick them good." Yet, about the time you have decided he is a knave, you meet some Indian he has been feeding for years, some lost man he has saved from death and given a bill of grub.

He comes from a time when kings were kings, and valiant knights rode the country in armor, fighting every warrior they met. He is the last of the errant knights, equally ready for a fight or a frolic; high-headed, intolerant, not even a natural leader but a lone warrior, out to battle with them all. To be friends with a man like that you have got to be humble, willing to listen a lot and talk very little, to respect him for what he is. And if his anger turns against you, that is rather a compliment. Most people he does not notice at all.

But about the time the world had forgotten Scotty he came out of his retirement with a roar. The papers all announced that he was going to build a castle—the finest in America, of course. He had already built one castle, away back in 1923, and torn it down again. It was a two-story plaster building, about forty by eighty, and had been built without benefit of architecture. It was just a huge warehouse, but it looked good to Scotty—this Spanish Palace never has appealed to him.

In moments of grandeur he speaks of "my castle" and claims all the credit for its construction, but he doesn't know a flying buttress from a donjon keep, and he only tolerates the moat they dug around it. It would take all the water away from his alfalfa, and they would have to build a drawbridge, to boot. Architecturally, it would be perfect over in Europe—but Death Valley is too dry for moats. Or that is what Scotty thinks—and that isn't all he thinks, either.

In 1935, when the whole world was broke and even Johnson was badly bent, Scotty spoke from the heart. His castle was closed, the taxes were not paid, and still the unthinking tourists came pouring in, only to find the huge gate closed.

"Everybody keeps coming to my castle," he said, "and expecting me to take them in and feed them and show them the hundred thousand dollar room. Well, there is a big sign up in front of the gates:

THIS CASTLE IS CLOSED
POSITIVELY NO ADMITTANCE
—Scotty

"A man brought the Governor of a State to see me yesterday and I turned them away. When they asked something about a lunch for ten people I told them there was a hotel down at Furnace Creek now and they could eat there. If they didn't have a sandwich they were out of luck, because I have stopped feeding everybody.

"When I was building this castle, which gave employment to thousands of men and cost two million, two hundred thousand dollars, I gave away forty thousand meals to people who came to see it. But now that I am having trouble over the title and they are trying to take it away from me, nobody turns a hand.

"Well, it is the new system and I have changed, too. In the old days I knew every man for a thousand miles around and they were all welcome. Now I never see an old-timer and these people who come are just strangers to me. I've never seen them before and I'll never see them again. So why should I run a restaurant to feed them and show them all over my castle? Let the hotels that send them out give them a lunch— and be sure they bring enough gas. Every guy that comes to see me is just out—but he's got a big bottle on his hip.

"Don't spring any of that stuff on me now—I'm off of booze for life."

In the old days Scotty had positive views about hospitality and he was constantly giving grub, water, clothes, money, to people he found stranded on the desert. Indians, too, and old-timers in general. When he was living in a tent-house where his castle now stands he was the soul of Western hospitality, and nothing made him so sore as to be treated shabbily in return. One fall he was riding in to Barstow past the Chemical Hills when he met a man after his own heart, a jeweler from Los Angeles.

He was travelling in a swell automobile and told Scotty his camp was a few miles back—anything he needed, stop and help himself. Scotty thanked him and said all he needed was a little salt. But when he came to the camp he found two fancy-dress ladies in the big tent who scarcely glanced at him. One of them finally looked out and asked him what he wanted. He said, a little salt. A tall man with a Van Dyke beard came out, looked him over and said he didn't think they had any salt.

Scotty told him all right, he could keep his damned salt. He even told him what he could do with it, although there were ladies present. At this one of the women came out of her trance. She divined from his language that this must be the great Scotty himself and tried to pose him for a picture, but he turned his back on her. Then the tall man inquired if he knew where there was any water, and how much he would charge to guide them to it. They were going to use the salts in glazing, commercially, but would have to have water on the ground.

"Yes," said Scotty. "I know where there is a good spring, eleven miles from here, that will flow right to the spot. I will guide you to it for ten thousand dollars—take it or leave it. No, I won't even do that. I'll ride over there right now and locate it myself. Any time you want it that bad you can buy it back for twenty thousand dollars. And the next time a man asks you for a little salt—you'd better have it."

On his way into Barstow he met a fresh motion picture director with a party of actors, out looking for a location. The director did nothing to soothe his wounded feelings but, after making some crack, asked him where he was from.

"I'm from hell and I'm going to hell," answered Scotty. "Where the hell are you from?"

With that he rode on, still talking to himself and still out of salt.

Life is like that with Scotty and, ever since his castle has been finished, it is one bunch of dudes after another. Some are fine and he shows them all over the place, and then somebody comes along who offends his proud spirit and he retires down the canyon in a huff. For two or three days he lives at his "hide-out," reading and feeding molasses to his fat little dog which is always begging for more. Then he gets into his car, unlocks the gate and drives back to the castle.

Instead of rising from some crag, as so many do in Europe, Scotty's Castle is built in the bottom of a canyon; but that does not detract from the beauty of its lines nor the brooding splendor of its patio. This is a spacious court, lying between the two wings of the palace, roofed over with bare poles which support wild clematis and the native grapevines of the canyon. Hand-wrought grilles and barred windows give a mediaeval effect and the sun-dial against one wall registers the time by a black finger on the dial. Every door is supported by elaborate hinges that spread out in intricate patterns until the whole surface is covered.

It is all solid concrete, plastered over with variegated stuccos, roofed with bright red tiles, its lines broken by deep-set windows. Built for a hot country, its exterior is a trifle severe; but once inside the door the whole vista changes. The floors are paved with tiles in dull red, green and yellow, each one with some ancient, heraldic design which harks back to the Middle Ages. Every piece of furniture is ornate to a degree, with elaborate metal chandeliers suspended from groined ceilings, all hand-carved and stained as with age.

These rooms are not the work of American mechanics but of old-world artisans, imported at great expense to give it the Continental touch. Fourteen giant fireplaces rise at the ends of long rooms, rich with curtains and tapestry, carpeted deep with rugs from the island of Majorca, in the Mediterranean.

Coming in from the raw desert, the effect of this splendor is dazzling. There is almost too much beauty for the walls to hold, and yet each room has a glory of its own. Many an old castle in Italy and Spain has given up its carved chairs and tables to make these bed-chambers more perfect, and the music-room is almost ecclesiastical.

But to possess all these things, and at a time when the financial world is coming down around our ears, is not an unmixed blessing. Mr. Johnson is a man of affairs, having had thousands of people dependent upon him since the wheels of industry half stopped. He has had other and more important things to do than worry about Scotty's Castle. It was really an incubus, an unprofitable expense—and yet the sightseers came on.

Scotty's Castle was begun as a rich man's retreat, where Mr. and Mrs. Johnson could retire for the winter and enjoy the simple life. But before it was half finished Death Valley was declared a National Monument; and, instead of a retreat, the castle became a show-place, with rubberneck busses at the gate. It would cost a small fortune to keep it open and show all the visitors through, so the problem was solved by charging admission as they do in most castles in Europe. But this is only a temporary solution, and far from the simple life.

When the castle was being built the Indians swarmed in and helped do the rough work; but Old Doc, their chief medicine man, was cynical.

"No good," he said. "Too big for live in. Pretty soon Hiko Man go, Injun move in. Squaw upstairs—horse downstairs."

That was his guess, but Doc was wrong. The *Indians* have all gone and the tourists have moved in. But Scotty lives on in his proud castle on the desert, and the crowds have come to *Him*. Perhaps it is his destiny always to be a showman—the one and only Scotty.

The End

[*117*]

I Remember Dane Coolidge

by Nancy Coolidge Coulter

Born at South Natick, Massachusetts, March 24, 1875, Dane Coolidge could look back over a long line of New England forebears to John and Mary Coolidge, who came from England in 1630. However, early in life (age about three or four) he became a "Westerner", when his parents brought him, his younger brother, and two sisters to the raw, new little town of Riverside in Southern California in search of a warm dry climate to benefit his Mother's "consumption". Unfortunately, it was too late. When Dane was seven or eight, his Mother died. His sisters also succumbed to tuberculosis, and Dane and his brother Herbert were raised by their Father in a womanless household.

Dane (christened Daniel) graduated from Stanford University in 1898 and did postgraduate work at Harvard. A naturalist as well as a writer, he collected mammals, birds, and reptiles for several well-known institutions, including the British Museum. In 1906 he married Mary Elizabeth Burroughs Roberts, a graduate of Cornell with a PhD from Stanford, where she had also been associate professor of Sociology. Their home, "Dwight Way End" in Berkeley, was the last house up the hill, with sizeable grounds—perhaps a couple of acres—where they lived almost all of their married lives, wrote their books, and entertained their friends.

I first met them in 1932 or '33, after I married Dane's

nephew, Coit Coolidge. They had no children (Mary was 45 when they married), so their nephews and nieces formed a surrogate family. I was immediately warmly welcomed into this group. From 1933 on, we lived in the Bay Area and so saw them often. When our children came along, a Sunday afternoon visit to Aunt Mary and Uncle Dane became one of our favorite family outings.

Perched high on the hill, the house commanded a sweeping view of Berkeley, the Bay, and the San Francisco skyline. A wide deck-porch made a delightful place to sit in the afternoon, enjoying a cold drink and listening to one of Uncle Dane's yarns—he was full of them! Dane and Mary did not go in for conventional decorations for Christmas and other holidays, but for such occasions they would hang their beautiful collection of Indian blankets over the balcony rail, where they were brightly visible to everyone coming up the hill—a really festive display! They also owned beautiful antique Manchu robes, bought in China about 1920, which they used as "dress-up" clothes for special parties and entertainments.

When I knew them, Mary (Dane always called her "Lady") was a professor of Sociology at Mills College in Oakland. She was also a writer, the author of *Why Women Are So* (much ahead of its time in 1911), *The Chinese in California* and *The Rainmakers*. She and Dane collaborated on several books, including *The Navaho Indians* and *The Last of the Seris*, which was their last book. Dane himself wrote about 40 Western novels, and several non-fiction books about the West, one of which is *Death Valley Prospectors*. He and Mary visited Death Valley Scotty in his "castle" often on their trips to the Southwest, as they were long-time friends.

Dane and Mary worked out a comfortable and practical way of life for themselves. During the nine months of the school year, Mary taught and Dane wrote. They frequently entertained friends—artists, writers, musicians—at dinner. Aunt Mary was a wonderful cook; Uncle Dane washed the dishes, probably his only household chore except for bringing in wood for the enormous stone fireplace.

Dane's usual working schedule involved spending the morning in the garden, where he had long curving terraces planted with China lilies and many-colored irises. This was also his time to think about whatever book he was then working on. After lunch, he went to his small writing room—scarcely larger than a big closet, and furnished with a desk, chair and typewriter, pigeon-holes for manuscripts, and a few shelves of books. It was all business; there was no room for frivolity. Here he would write until dinner-time. About 8:00 or 8:30, after doing the dishes, he would return to this room and put in another two or three hours. The day's quota was 2,000 words, and this he did every working day, good or bad. If it was bad, it was revised later or discarded, but he always kept to his program of 2,000 words a day.

During the summer months, Dane and Mary traveled and camped throughout the Southwest, collecting stories, information and artifacts. Dane had a large Graflex camera, with which he took innumerable photographs of Indians, cowboys, wild horses, and the desert. He also kept meticulous notebooks, but the camera allowed him to pass as an itinerant photographer, as well as providing illustrations for his books. This way, he felt that the cowboys would not try to fill him up with "tall tales", as they might if he admitted to being a writer.

They followed this pattern of living and writing for many years, until old age and failing health forced them to slow down. Dane died in August, 1940; Mary, who was 12 years older, outlived him by five years. Theirs was a close and productive partnership; I feel privileged to have known them.

Index

Index

Index

Surprise Cyn: 55, 57, 58-59
Surveyor's Well: 17, 35, 96, 100, 101, 103

Teel's Marsh (Nev.) : 41
Tehuantepec: 70
Telescope Peak: 94
Texas: 49
Thurman, Old Man: 92, 93
Tilton, Frank: 39
Tin Mt: 101
Tonopah and Tidewater RR: 39
Tonopah, Nev: 88, 90, 94
Tucki Mt: 15, 35, 49
Tule Hole: 75, 76
Twenty-Mule Teams: 38, 39-40, 42

United States: 112

United States Geological Survey: 101

Warm Springs: 32, 33
Wellman, Harry: 58
Wells-Fargo Express Co: 55-57
Wells, Nev: 106
Wet Trail: 91
Wild Rose: 91, 92
Wild Rose Canyon: 34, 45
Wild West Show: 103, 106-108
Wilson, Tom: 14, 17, 31, 50
Winters, Aaron (& Rosie) : 38
Woodpecker Cyn: 58
World Beater Mine: 33, 95
World War (I) : 37, 85
Wrinkle, Charley: 82-84
Wyoming (Mine) : 56